ARCHITECTURE

THE PROFESSIONS

in preparation

Banking Evan Hughes
Medicine Jane Gray
Teaching John Watts

Contents

	Introduction	7
ONE	The Architect and His Collaborators	13
TWO	Private Practice and Public Service	30
THREE	The Professional Man	44
FOUR	What Kind of Person?	63
FIVE	Opportunities and Rewards	76
SIX	Learning Architecture	93
SEVEN	The Daily Round	105
EIGHT	A Look Ahead	121
	Appendices	135
	Bibliography	141
	Index	145

Introduction

It has been said that you can always tell an architect by his bow-tie. This is untrue, but like many wild generalisations it has an element of truth in it. It throws a little light on the kind of person an architect is, as well as on the kind of image he likes to present. Many architects, trained to be discriminating about appearances, have something of the dandy in them. They also have an instinct to do things in their own way and resist accepting the way other people do them, and they have an interest in practical techniques of all kinds, represented perhaps by their ability to tie a bow confidently and precisely. Minor idiosyncrasies of dress are many people's means of asserting some degree of independence from the norm. An architect wants to feel that he is nearer to the artist than to the businessman, and to compensate himself for having to spend less of his time actually being an artist than he would like.

One reason why he is sensitive about his image is that he is aware how little the public knows and understands of what he does and what his responsibilities are. Architecture is classed among the professions, which are defined thus in the *Concise Oxford Dictionary*: 'vocation, calling, esp. one that involves some branch of learning or science'. The public respects the architect for this but does not have a picture of him as a man with a central part to play in the organisation of society. The public tends—and this is what the architect particularly resents—to regard him as a luxury: someone who, though symbolising civilised living, can, as a matter of practical business, be done without.

It is difficult to prove the architect's indispensability to anyone unacquainted with the range of his activities (except sometimes by pointing out what has happened when attempts have been made to manage without him), because it is true that a builder—indeed anyone equipped with a small amount of practical sense—can put up a house without employing an architect (though whether he would be allowed to do so depends on the location; in some countries—not including Britain—employment of an architect, or at least the use of plans signed by an architect, is compulsory). But an architect can make a vast contribution to the quality of the house and reduce its cost and the time taken to build it, since he is concerned with siting, planning, constructional technique, finance and supervising the work of the builder, not merely with the final appearance of the building, although the last is what he is often judged by.

Houses, moreover, represent only a fraction of the building projects that occupy an architect's time, and the larger and more complex the building the more deeply is he involved in planning and constructional problems. He may even have to prepare the programmes on which his own designs are to be based. To take but one example: when an industrialist decides to build a new factory, it often falls to the architect to look at the old one and analyse the processes that take place in it, to study the sequence of operations from the delivery of raw materials to the despatch of the finished products, so that he can plan a building in which all these operations will take place more efficiently.

His responsibilities, in addition, merge into town planning and even into sociology, since the process of designing a housing scheme, for example, should not be separated from consideration of the type and arrangement of accommodation that will best suit the future occupants, and into property finance when he advises developers about the potentialities of sites. He also has even wider

8

responsibilities to the public as a whole, and must balance the interests of the client for whom he is designing a building against the public interest that may be affected by its siting or the way it is used or what it looks like. This is one of his obligations as a professional man, and the present-day concern about the environment has led to his being increasingly criticised if he does not fulfil such obligations conscientiously.

He is expected not only to design efficient and good-looking buildings, but buildings that improve rather than harm their surroundings. For architects are in the awkward position of being at the same time among the principal agencies through which the environment changes—as change it must—and among the agencies with a special duty to safeguard it, and although a deteriorating environment can often be blamed on factors with which architects have nothing to do, there are some who must take a share of the blame. For example there are architects who will carry through any job regardless of whether it is socially or environmentally desirable (by being, for instance, too big for its site or on a badly chosen site) either because they conceive their loyalty to be only to the client who has employed them or because they want the work and the fees it will bring, and tell themselves that if they refuse the job someone less scrupulous will certainly be found to undertake it. Such architects, though often the eminent and commercially successful ones, are still fortunately in the minority.

To some extent architects and those who employ them are restrained from putting their and their clients' interests before those of the community by the planning legislation that has grown up as building activities have expanded and the pressures these bring to bear on the environment have become more of a problem. Legislation of this kind is more strict and comprehensive in some countries than in others. Britain has very advanced legislation (though the results are not always as satisfactory as this would lead one to hope), and architects and their institutions did much to bring the British planning laws into being. Architects have also been prominent among those who have led the fight against the irresponsible destruction of historic buildings and against spoiling by insensitive new buildings the established character of towns and villages.

At this point I should make it clear that this book describes architecture as practised in Britain. The art of architecture is of course international, since its purposes are the same everywhere. Differences lie in some countries, when they are technically and industrially more advanced than others, having greater resources, and there are many differences in the way the architectural profession is organised and administered. For example in some countries the roles of the architect and the engineer are hardly separated. In others architects can also serve as contractors, and therefore have neither the status nor the obligations of the professional man.

In countries that are highly developed industrially, like America and most of the European countries, the position of the architect is nevertheless much the same as in Britain, and therefore the discussions of his activities and problems on the following pages have a general application. But practice also differs in many details, and these I have not attempted to go into.

The activities of the architect are restricted in countries where he is classed as a professional man by strict rules of conduct imposed by his own institutions—in the case of Britain by the Royal Institute of British Architects and by the Architects' Registration Council. He is obliged to obey these rules or risk being struck off the register.

Another of the traditional roles of the architect is to hold a balance between the interests of the client for whom he has designed a building and those of the building contractor who is to put it up, seeing that each gets fair treatment and a reasonable bargain. But the character of this role is changing. In the days when the client was a moneyed gentleman and the builder a mere tradesman, and it was assumed that the latter was likely to be a rogue from whose dishonesties the client had to be protected, one of the architect's main jobs was to make sure that work was not scamped and that the materials used were those that had been specified and paid for. Nowadays a building contract is more often between one businessman and another, and new building techniques and the importance of saving time and economising labour demand that their relationship should be one of collaboration instead of mutual suspicion. Nevertheless, the principle of *caveat emptor* (let the buyer look after his own interests) still applies, since builders, sub-contractors and suppliers of materials, though mostly honest men, are naturally out to make what profit they can. The buyer of the services a builder provides—that is, the architect's client—has neither the time nor the expert knowledge to look after his own interests. To do so on his behalf is the architect's responsibility; and so the architect must see that the client gets what he has paid for, but at the same time he must see that the process of putting up a building is fair to everyone concerned—client, builder and the public. The architect is not bound, like many clients and all contractors, by the ordinary code of commercial morality but by his own professional code of ethics.

I have mentioned the changing relationship between architect, client and builder at this point to indicate the way the architect's job is continually being influenced by new developments of all kinds, social and technical, so that he is now hardly recognisable as the same person who was first given the name of architect 300 years or so ago, though his original role is that on which his public image is still based.

CHAPTER ONE

The Architect and His Collaborators

Since this is not a history book, there is no need to recount in detail the story of the gradual emergence of the architect as we know him from the master-builder who had the main responsibility for the design and construction of medieval churches, cathedrals and palaces but who left much to the initiative of individual craftsmen. The architect who succeeded him—it is not until the seventeenth century that the names and personalities of architects become generally identifiable—was still dependent on craftsmen. Masons, carpenters, carvers and cabinet-makers were given a great deal of latitude in the execution of details, and clerks of works took charge of construction on the site.

The architect was a scholar and a man of taste, without academic training in architecture and often simply concerned with following the newest fashions; but exceptionally he was also a man of ideas, through whose imagination and interest in experiment the art of architecture was pushed forward as a part of the scientific and philosophical developments that were taking place at this time. He was sometimes an amateur in the ancient sense of a man deeply involved in the culture of his time, of which architecture was only one manifestation—and one not yet organised into a separate compartment. Christopher Wren began as an astronomer and was one of the founders of the Royal Society, a learned scientific body such as no architect would aspire to belong to today. Vanbrugh was a playwright as well as an architect, and the Earl of Burlington, a century later, was both architect and an influential patron of architecture.

Throughout the eighteenth century, however, the architect became increasingly a professional man, and by the beginning of the nineteenth the type of architect we know, with an office and a corps of draughtsmen, was firmly established. He no longer had the same personal relationship with the craftsmen, who were under the control of the builder, and the architect gave his instructions to the builder by means of elaborate sets of drawings, himself paying only occasional visits to the site.

Everything now centred on one man, which may have made for efficiency—if the man was efficient—but which tended to isolate the art of architecture from practical developments in constructional technique and was one of the reasons why it lost touch with reality when vast changes, technical and social, began to make new demands on it. At the same time the architect acquired a fully professional status, supported by all the apparatus of professionalism like institutes, libraries and codes of professional conduct (the Institute of British Architects was founded in 1834 and was given its Royal Charter three years later). He became widely accepted as a gentleman; and the tendency more and more to interest himself in aspects of his art that could be discussed with other gentlemen—in questions of scholarship and antiquarian precedent and in the niceties of successively fashionable styles—again unfitted him to adjust himself to changes that were eventually to shake the foundations of his world.

This type of skilful, dedicated and socially superior professional man lasted for more than a century. He had many admirable qualities, but during this period a great many needs arose, such as mass housing (due to the sudden growth of cities) and factories and docks and railway stations (due to the growth of industry and new transport systems, following the Industrial Revolution and the expansion of the British Empire) which his experience did not equip him to design even had he wished to involve himself in tasks he regarded as inartistic. In addition, new techniques, resulting from the introduction into building of iron and steel and later concrete, opened up new possibilities of many kinds which his limitations of outlook and training prevented him from exploiting. He got increasingly out of touch with significant developments, almost to the point where, except as a designer of churches, rich men's mansions and civic monuments, he was looked on as a luxury rather than a necessity. For the last fifty years he has been striving to put this right.

Today the architect is still a strictly organised professional man, but other professions have grown up alongside his own, and with some of these he finds himself in a difficult relationship because of the history recounted above and because of his continuing efforts to reassume the responsibilities from which he abdicated a century ago. The chief of these professions is that of the engineers, with whom the architect is still involved in destructive and unnecessary rivalry—unnecessary because each has his contribution to make and there is room and need for both.

Engineers, as a body of men trained in certain skills and with a fund of inherited experience, are of course older than architects. They descend from the specialists in military fortifications, through the builders of bridges and utilitarian structures of all kinds, down to the time when the complex and multifarious techniques they had to master caused them to split up into their present many branches: civil, structural, mechanical, electrical, railway, aeronautical, heating and ventilating and many other engineers. But at times in their history, what we now call civil engineers have been indistinguishable from architects—in fact they have been one and the same thing. Who can say whether the master-builder who devised the complex structure of a medieval cathedral should be called an architect or an engineer?

Specialisation was an inevitable outcome of a more complex

civilisation. The barber-surgeon became half a dozen different kinds of doctor and the clerk even more different kinds of civil servant and local authority official; and it was reasonable for the master-builder or architect-engineer to divide himself into the man who seeks order and harmony as well as convenience in buildings and the man who is technically expert at constructing them.

We can thus say that the architect is distinguished by being an artist or visionary, and the engineer by being essentially a practical man; yet in good architecture designing and constructing are inseparable, which means that both engineer and architect have to be practical and visionary at the same time, whatever legitimate bias each may have in one of these directions. The architectural profession went astray at the time of the Industrial Revolution by not only ignoring the practical resources newly made available to it, but by confining its visionary role within familiar and un-adventurous limits. It was the engineers who saw visions of what the new technologies could achieve and the changes they would bring, both in the demand for new buildings and in how the demand could be met. Inspired by the challenge the age presented to them, engineers designed—invented is perhaps a better word—structures like docks and train-sheds, bridges and viaducts, that are among the most notable of their time. Men like Robert Stephenson, Telford and the younger Brunel were the true architects, in the sense of constructors with real vision, of the early years of the nineteenth century.

While such men were endowing Britain—and by their example the world—with structures of a scale and a noble simplicity that had not been seen since Roman times, the professional architects were content to apply their talents to esoteric variations on a succession of styles and fashions. They were called in if the promoter of a building wanted to make a show, to dress it up in some picturesque or status-giving style. The best architects produced fascinating buildings of much charm and interest to the connoisseur, but buildings increasingly remote from satisfying the needs of a rapidly changing civilisation.

The transformation of nearly every country in the Western world which accompanied the processes of industrialisation and urbanisation was thus principally the work of engineers. They equipped industry and transport with the multifarious new types of building these processes demanded, while unlettered contractors provided the close-packed acres of housing for their workers. Since the architects had shown no interest—as designers let alone as planners—in the problems the new developments presented, they, together with industry's heartless philistinism and its exploitation of cheap labour, must take much of the responsibility for the slums that it has needed nearly a century to eradicate.

By the time architects at last realised how disastrously, both for society and for the art of architecture, they had removed themselves from the live issues of the day, they had a long way to catch up, and the significance of the architectural revolution that took place in Britain and America in the 1920s and 1930s (following the lead that had been set on the Continent of Europe a decade earlier) was not simply that it discarded the imitations of historic styles which had become increasingly meaningless in relation to the new building requirements and materials and techniques; it was not even that architects at last began to discover what marvellous things the new techniques could achieve. Its significance was that architects took a fresh look at the role they could play in bringing order and humanity into an increasingly chaotic world—and found that it was a key role.

In this sense modern architecture, as it came to be called, represented far more than a change in style (though the aesthetic outcome of the revolution did help to make architecture obviously belong to the new machine-dominated world). It represented a new interest on the architects' part in the land and how it should be planned, in cities and how they should grow, in people and how they should be housed. This arose both from their social conscience and from their professional ambition. It had become clear that a great many of the deficiencies that met the eye at every turn in the industrialised Western world, such as the uncontrolled spread of cities, poor housing standards, unhealthy working conditions and the despoliation of the open countryside, could only be remedied by employing those skills that the architect—and no one else—was trained to provide. These included an ability to keep the whole picture in his mind while other professionals and technicians were concentrating on particular details, and to hold a balance between private wishes and the public good; in fact to be what we call nowadays an environmentalist.

Of course by no means all architects suddenly changed their habits and attitudes. It is too easy, when writing about developments in architecture—in fact in writing history of any kind—to discuss the doings of the significant minority by whom history is made as if they were typical. Many architects carried on in the same old way—some are doing so still—perhaps adopting minor changes in style so as not to appear out of date. But a seed had at least been implanted, and as it slowly germinated within the profession it changed the whole approach to architecture in two key places: in the professional institutes and in the architectural schools. The programmes and activities of both have been based ever since on recognition of the need for architecture to accept its social responsibilities.

This it is now better geared to do. Nevertheless, the legacy of the time when engineers were in charge of nearly all the building that was altering the balance of society is with us still. There are many types of building, from factories to suburban housing estates, in which the architect has no part; or if he is not completely excluded, his role is to add some trimmings after the real planning and designing have been done. Engineers, too, have kept the superior place in the various administrative hierarchies that they earned for themselves in the nineteenth century. In local government every borough has its engineer, but only sometimes is there a borough architect, and if there is one his department may simply be a branch of the engineer's. In organisations like the railways, architecture is classed as a branch of engineering, and all over the world Public Works Departments, following the pattern set in the nineteenth century, are staffed by engineers with architects at a lower level helping to implement policies formulated by engineers. Architects may complain about this for reasons of status, but it is not only they but the environment that suffers. To say so is not to disparage the engineer as a man with a useful—indeed a vital—contribution to make; for to say that the cart must not be put before the horse is not to deny the usefulness of the cart. But the engineer is a specialist, concentrating like other specialists on his own particular skills, whereas no one but the architect includes among his skills that of embracing the general, rather than the particular, view. His job is to understand what is needed and work out how it can best be provided, but at the same time to keep an eye on what the ultimate outcome of his and his collaborators' efforts will be like as a contribution to the environment. That is why he must be allowed to deploy his talents at the only stage of any building operation when they can be fully effective—at the beginning.

To put it another way, the architect, whom the public persists in regarding as someone concerned mainly with aesthetics, has emerged in the twentieth century as, more than anything else, a planner. His main job is the creation of order, and as civilisation grows more complex, and as more and more users compete for the diminishing amount of building land, it becomes essential to plan well ahead so as to use it in the best and most orderly way. This has extended the architect's planning responsibilities into wider fields, a subject I shall have to discuss shortly.

The complexity of modern life has also placed a new emphasis on his role as the planner of buildings. Architects have always been concerned with the plans of buildings as well as their appearance, and in past centuries have at times laid out sequences of streets and even whole quarters of towns for land-owners or the Crown. But this was in the days when requirements were obvious and planning problems relatively simple. No expert investigation was needed to discover how a terrace of houses was going to be lived in or how the church that closed the view at the end of the terrace was going to be used. Today the architect with, for example, a hospital to design must begin by familiarising himself with every detail of the working of the hospital. Only when he knows what goes on in each department can he allot to it the space it needs and decide how it can be most conveniently related to the other departments. He must listen to the ideas of everyone in charge of a department, to learn how he wants his wards or operating theatres or laboratories or kitchens arranged. These people may have clear ideas of what they want; on the other hand the architect, with his experience of analysing relationships and creating a logical pattern out of them, may be able to suggest still better arrangements. Ideally he should talk to patients and nurses and cleaning staff and visitors as well as to doctors and management.

Only when all this preliminary work has been done, when relationships have been worked out and space allocated, can the architect discuss with the hospital management such fundamental questions as whether the departments should be piled up into a small number of multi-storey buildings or be spread over the site in the form of lower connected buildings, and only then can the process of devising a physical shape for the building begin and its architectural character emerge. Whether a building is as complicated as a hospital or more straightforward like a block of offices or a cinema, it will be a better building for having gone through this exacting process. In fact one way of defining the difference between the way the modern architect designs and the way his grandfather designed is to say that today the visible form, and therefore the aesthetic quality, of a building emerge as part of the process of solving practical problems, whereas architects before tended to begin with a picture of the final result and adapt the functional needs to it. This does not mean that modern design grows automatically out of functional considerations. It allows plenty of opportunity for exercise of the imagination and for aesthetic judgement; but such judgements cannot be separated from all the other decisions which the structure will eventually reflect.

If the research, analysis and consultations with others that the architect has to undertake while designing many types of individual building have become so complex, how much more so is the process of designing on a really large scale. Planning a housing estate or a new town, and especially planning the future growth and the adaptation to changing needs of an existing town, involve sociological, financial, administrative and transport questions far outside the normal tasks of the architect. It is to deal with these that the separate town-planning profession has been established; yet the architect's part in all such tasks remains vital.

When the confusion that was overtaking towns and cities—and indeed the countryside as well—became so evident at the beginning of this century that some system of planning ahead, some machinery for controlling the use of land and the siting of buildings in the public interest, were obviously necessary, the architects were the first practitioners of the new science. It was a natural extension of their traditional activities; they were the first to press for control to be exercised over the increasingly chaotic background against which they had to work, and there was no one else with their experience of analysing social needs and providing three-dimensional answers to them.

At first, therefore, town planning was mostly done by architects spending some or all of their time dealing with the larger picture—with planning groups of buildings instead of individual buildings—and when it became established as a separate profession, most of those who adopted it were architects. Until only a few years ago there were no separate schools for training town planners; only courses in planning available in the schools of architecture. Town planning (or town and country planning as it is properly called, since it deals with the total environment, rural as well as urban—and the other areas which are neither one nor the other, of which there are far too many) is now recognised as a separate profession, and town planners are recruited not only from those with an architectural training but from those with more of a bias towards surveying, sociology or estate management. Yet the architect's discriminating eye, his concern for the appearance of things, is an essential part of the practising town planner's equipment. Much has been lost as a result of the administration of our elaborate town-planning laws being largely in the hands of bureaucrats who lack visual imagination and have no basis of training or experience on which to judge visual relationships.

However separate they are professionally, close collaboration between town planners and architects is therefore important if the final result is to turn out satisfactorily, and it is also important to the architect in his practice because it is through the town planners in official positions that he makes sure that the designs on which he is working conform to planning requirements and are acceptable environmentally.

There are a few town planners working privately, mostly as consultants of some kind, but by far the largest number of qualified town planners (leaving aside those practising architects who also have town-planning degrees) work for central or local government authorities. The administrative machinery for controlling land-use, instituted earlier this century, which I have already referred to, was the outcome of a series of Acts of Parliament, and amendments to them, the most far-reaching of which was the Town and Country Planning Act of 1947. This legislation obliges each local government authority designated as a planning authority (which means all the county councils and county borough councils) to appoint a planning officer.* His job is to see that planning regulations are conformed with, as well as to formulate long-term plans for the development of his area. In practice, most planning officers are too busy operating the day-

* The forthcoming reorganisation of local government in Britain may include the reallocation of planning responsibilities, and there is a danger of some planning being delegated to bodies too small to be able to afford to employ experienced professional planners.

to-day statutory controls to give enough time to constructive forward planning; nor do the committees of the elected councils, to whom planning officers are responsible, take as much initiative about this as they should. The long-term picture, instead of being foreseen, is too often simply the result of a succession of *ad-hoc* decisions.

One of the planning officer's principal tasks is to deal with applications for planning permission. Every proposal for a new building, or for changing the use of an existing one, has to be submitted to him by the architect so that he can examine it and only grant permission, without which no building operation may go ahead, if the project suits local requirements. Obtaining planning permission often involves the architect in long discussions and negotiations, because the planning Acts enable local authorities not only to control matters like use-zoning (that is, restricting factory building to particular areas or deciding what kind of building other than houses can be allowed in a mainly residential area) and the density at which a site may be built over and how high a building may go; they also allow control of shape, colour and materials, and planning permission can be withheld if any of these are thought unsuitable for their surroundings.

Architects naturally resent it if this happens. They do not like their aesthetic decisions to be questioned by an official with no architectural qualfications; they are also sometimes apprehensive lest this should affect their own standing with their client. Appeal against the refusal of planning permission can be made to the central government, but even if successful this results in delays, which again are not likely to be popular with clients.

Nevertheless, it is right that local authorities should have these comprehensive planning powers because there must be some way of dealing with all the showy, illiterate and gimcrack buildings that create so much ugliness if control is not exercised. The unfortunate thing is that bad building—badly designed as well as badly sited—continues in spite of the existence of controls theoretically capable of preventing it. It usually means that the

planning officer and his committee are too busy to examine proposals properly, have no aesthetic judgement or do not care; or
timidity may lead them to reject only what they find unfamiliar,
thereby perpetuating the kind of development that exists already
and penalising initiative and originality.

Many poor quality buildings are, of course, not designed by
architects,* and it has been suggested that projects by qualified
architects should be made exempt from control on aesthetic
grounds. This would be sensible if all architects were good
architects, which is unfortunately not the case. Another way of
getting over the difficulty of control being exercised by officials
without architectural training has been tried in several localities:
this is the appointment, by the local authority's planning committee, of a panel of local architects to whom designs can be
referred for an opinion on their aesthetic merits. There are,
however, obvious disadvantages in architects sitting in judgement on each other's designs, and since it tends to be the senior
architects who are invited to serve on the panels—men, very
likely, with fixed ideas—there is again prejudice against the un-
orthodox.

But all the blame for the unsatisfactory operation of planning
controls must not be assigned to planning officers (or even to the
political and financial policies of the councils they serve, which
naturally have a powerful influence on plans and their imple-
mentation). Some of the blame must rest with the architects.
Architects have always approved of the principle behind town
planning: that individual buildings should be related and co-
ordinated so that the larger scene has virtues of its own over and
above the virtues of each building, so that the public good is
considered as well as private gain and so that future needs can be
foreseen and planned for. But they are not always willing to sup-

---

* In round figures Britain spends £3,150 million a year on building,
of which between 15 and 20 per cent is not handled at any stage by
architects.

port the principle when their own interests or preferences are at stake.

They may feel, mistakenly, that loyalty to their client obliges them to do their best to make sure that he gets his way even if what he wants is contrary to the public interest; they may be arrogant enough to assume that their designs are beyond criticism; they may simply be too obstinate to be prepared to make changes. Whatever the reason, conflict between architect and planning officer is accepted by too many architects as the normal relationship, and he acquires the habit of regarding the process of seeking and obtaining planning permission as just one more of the bureaucratic obstacles that have to be overcome before he can start building. 'I've got it through planning' is his way of putting it.

This may to some extent merely reflect the frustrations and delays he becomes involved in because of the cumbersome procedures of the planning laws; but it also suggests a failure to remember that town planning is an extension of architecture and that the objectives his professional obligations require him to seek make many of his activities subservient to those of the planner. The architect's relationship with the town planner is thus partly based on the fact that they share the same skills, and partly on the fact that they are allied professions, requiring mutual co-operation. As architects become more aware of their duty to the environment, the dividing line between architecture and town planning becomes more difficult to draw and the need for co-operation between the two professions inescapable.

I have already said something about the architect's other principal collaborator, the engineer, and about the sometimes delicate relationship between them arising from their past history and from the fact that the two professions were once one. But in spite of continuing rivalry in certain fields of operation, architects and engineers work closely together on the design of all kinds of buildings. When the building is a modest one, like a house, the architect will probably feel able to deal with the structural

25

problems without calling in an engineer, though he may do so if the design includes large spaces that have to be specially roofed or if there are difficult soil conditions requiring special foundations. But with larger buildings the alternative methods of construction and the materials available are so many, and the calculations involved in using them so complex, that a specialist is nearly always needed.

The architect must consult with the structural engineer from the very beginning. The days have gone when he made a design and then asked the engineer to tell him how to build it. The form of a modern building is often partly dictated by the means chosen to construct and roof it, and the architect and engineer decide on these jointly as the design is worked out from the volumes and spaces required.

There are other specialists besides the structural engineer, who may or may not be called in according to the complexity of the job: the heating engineer (though a simple heating and hot water system for domestic use is often designed, under the architect's supervision, by the heating contractor who is going to install it); the ventilating engineer (usually from the same firm of consultants as the heating engineer) when the building is to have artificial ventilation or air-conditioning; the acoustic engineer, the lighting engineer and several more. With these, too, early consultation is important; and buildings dependent on a large number of services, like hospitals, factories, scientific institutions and hotels, may be planned to a great extent round the most efficient and economical arrangement of all the ducts, pipes and cables that these services require.

There are at least two other professional men with whom the architect of a building may need to collaborate during the design process, one concerned with the larger spaces around it and the other with the spaces enclosed by it. These are the landscape architect and the interior designer. Landscape architecture, as distinct from landscape gardening, has emerged as a separate profession even more recently than town planning. The role of the landscape architect needs no description. As control of the environment becomes more necessary, his expertise in ground-shaping and planting becomes more important. The interior designer is in a somewhat different category because he might better be described as a special kind of architect.

As often as not, the architect is himself responsible for the interiors and the furnishing of his buildings, and it is reasonable that he should argue that the whole building, inside and out, ought to be seen as one design, and that he should object to some-one else deciding, for example, what colour the walls should be painted. But there is a case for making interior design a specialised study, especially in buildings with peculiar problems that need experience to solve, or which depend on keeping up with chang-ing fashions—buildings like shops, restaurants and cinemas. The specialist interior designer (who need not be a qualified architect because he has no need also to be a planner and constructor) is another inescapable product of the growing complexity of the architect's job and the varying demands it makes on him. A man with a talent for analysing and planning for a sequence of manu-facturing operations has not necessarily a good eye for colour; a man with the spatial imagination to design a cathedral cannot necessarily design an armchair.

Finally, one other specialist with whom the architect has to collaborate must be mentioned, but this time one who is not involved in the planning or appearance of the building but in estimating its cost and making sure this is kept to. He is the quantity surveyor, a man of whose work the general public is almost unaware but who, in large buildings especially, has a big part to play in the procedure of getting them economically and expeditiously built. From the architect's drawings the quantity surveyor calculates the materials and labour required and helps the architect estimate the cost. It is on the basis of his figures that the builder submits his prices. He checks and values the work done by the builder so that payments can be made at proper intervals. He also makes himself useful to the architect with advice about the cost of alternative forms of construction or of using different materials; yet it is sometimes suggested that the quantity surveyor has build himself up into a seemingly indispensable part of the vast and complicated building machine without sufficient justification. It is noteworthy that in America the quantity surveyor is not known, yet building is efficient and cost very important. In America the building contractor does the calculations about quantities of materials (which he also does in Britain, while working out his prices, thus duplicating to a large extent the work of the quantity surveyor) and costs in America do not seem to get out of control.

The multiplicity of consultants and collaborators described above may suggest that the architect has become part of so complicated a team effort as to leave him with little scope for initiative and individuality. This is indeed true as regards some types of large building enterprises, but the curbs on his freedom of action do not result from the number of fellow professionals on whose specialised skills he is dependent so much as from the cumulative effect of bylaws, fire regulations and planning and other restriction, intended to protect the public but often too inflexibly administered or too out of touch with new technical developments. In any case the architect retains a controlling position in the modern building team because it is normally he who chooses, or advises on the choice of, the individuals in other professions who are to collaborate with him, as well as the contractor who is to carry out the work.

Some kinds of architectural practice undoubtedly require a greater variety of knowledge and experience than one man can encompass, and this has led to the establishment of large partnerships and, more experimentally, of partnerships in which several professions are represented. The obvious advantage of the large architectural partnership is that it offers the maximum chance of all the various talents required being found somewhere among the partners. It also provides an opportunity for lifting some members of the firm above the status of mere employees and giving them a stake in the firm's prosperity. Architects want to keep a successful team together, and one way of persuading a valued assistant not to move on to another firm, or set up on his own, is to make him a partner or at least to raise him to a position of all-round responsibility approaching that of a partner, for whom the term associate is generally used.

The relationship between employer and employed within the architectural profession I shall pursue in another chapter, but the ambitious experiment of forming multi-professional partnerships, with architects, engineers, landscape architects, town planners and quantity surveyors working together in the same firm, clearly belongs to this one. Its advantages are obvious: since all these people have constantly to be consulted during the course of a job, why not bring them together under the same roof so that they become accustomed to working together and form, in effect, a multi-disciplinary team?

This sounds progressive, and several partnerships of this kind have been formed, usually with the architect taking the initiative. But there are many who disagree with the idea. What the architect wants, they argue, when the need arises to call in an engineer, for example, or a town planner, is the best available engineer or town planner for the particular job to be done. 'How unlikely it is,' they say, 'that the best man should happen to be the very man whom I have joined up with in my own partnership. I prefer to feel that I have the maximum freedom of choice.'

CHAPTER TWO

Private Practice and Public Service

The architect discussed in the preceding chapter resembles his ancestor of some centuries ago in still being an independent professional man who takes his instructions direct from the client and gets his living by the fees his client pays him. This traditional figure still in some respects dominates the profession, and he is foremost in the public eye because he is still the designer of most prominent buildings; but he is nevertheless today in a minority. During the past half-century the architectural profession has been almost revolutionised by the increase in numbers and influence of a different kind of figure, the salaried architect—and especially the architect employed in the public service.

As a result of this, and as a result of the increased size of private partnerships employing large numbers of qualified architects, more than 70 per cent of all architects are now in salaried employment rather than being their own masters. This has done more than anything to create a different image for the architect from that of the somewhat dilettante artistic gentleman current a short time ago—as described in the introductory chapter of this book—and the profession is still adapting itself to this change. The architectural schools, however, have hardly begun to do so. Their teaching methods still appear to assume that every student's ambition and destiny is an office of his own with a brass plate with his name on it beside the door.

The growth of salaried employment is partly, as explained above, the result of the growing complexity of architectural practice giving rise to large firms with many assistants, but far more is it the result of the setting up of large architectural offices by both central and local governments—something that is new in our generation. The employment of architects by the state is not new—Wren was Surveyor of Works (the title given in his time to the nation's chief architect) under four successive monarchs, and so later were Chambers, Adam and other famous men. What is new is the transfer to public and municipal authorities of the responsibility for certain important categories of building, notably schools and to a great extent housing, and the consequent establishment of official architects' departments woven into the fabric of local government.

These departments employ in Britain roughly 40 per cent of all the architects there are (see table in Appendix 2), and this relatively new development has meant, in effect, that the architect's work has been recognised as a social service. It ought to mean also, but does not always do so, that architecture can be much more closely linked with other related public services: that the design of housing, for example, can be linked in day-to-day practice with matters like rent and management, and the design of schools with educational policy; also that both can be better tied in with the local authority's land-use and development plans, especially since official architectural offices have grown up side by side with the official departments responsible for town planning.

The opportunity of co-ordinating the work of social and territorial planners with that of the architect is one obvious advantage of establishing him as a part of local government machinery. Another advantage is the opportunity it gives him of building up experience of a particular type of problem over a long period. Private architects are usually switching their attention all the time between different kinds of building and may tackle one kind only once in their whole career. A public office—say that of a county council, which is responsible for all the schools in its area*—tackles one school after another. It has the opportunity of applying to each the lessons learnt from the previous ones and of gradually building up a fund of experience on which everyone working in the office can draw.

The defects of the public architectural office—or so it has always been said—are the ones common to all large bureaucratic organisations: a tendency towards sluggishness, an insistence on conforming to established rules and procedures and a resultant loss of initiative. These characteristics are indeed fatal to good architecture, but are not necessarily the outcome of architecture being organised as an activity of a public authority. Designing buildings is a process that involves continually taking decisions, and not necessarily decisions that can be arrived at simply by following precedent. Therefore, if initiative is to be maintained within a bureaucratic framework, the structure of the office must be such that architectural decisions—as distinct from policy decisions—are left to the architect in charge of each project instead of having to be referred higher up as is customary in most bureaucracies.

That such a work structure is possible was demonstrated at the end of the 1940s at the London County Council. The council had a very large architect's department, employing a couple of hundred architects and responsible for a quantity of work in the London area: housing, schools of all grades, fire and ambulance stations, magistrates' courts and many kinds of public building. Like other large public offices at the time, which ranged from the chief architect's department of the Ministry of Works, responsible for all the building work of central government (and therefore the

* The forthcoming reorganisation of local government, referred to in the preceding chapter, may change the present allocation of responsibility for housing, schools etc, and thus the level at which the public architectural offices operate.

descendant of the Surveyor's office of which Wren had been in charge), down to the relatively small architectural offices of the lesser borough councils, the LCC office suffered from many of the bureaucratic defects I have just indicated. Moreover, because the work in public offices involved much routine and was thought to be dull, if worthy, and to offer few chances of individual initiative, the architects who chose to work in them were chiefly those interested in a safe job with a pension at the end of it. Promotion was by seniority more than merit, and the men who reached the top were nearing the end of their careers, were set in their ways and were attached to whatever was well tried and familiar. This may not have been true at the top of every public office, but it was the prevailing pattern.

In the LCC this pattern became transformed after Sir Robert Matthew was appointed architect to the council in 1949. He replaced what might be called a horizontal work structure, in which everyone did the jobs appropriate to his level and only began to take real responsibility when he rose to near the top, with a vertical structure which allowed each architect or group of architects to take the whole responsibility for the particular building they worked on, seeing it through from beginning to end. In effect the architects in the department were divided into groups, each of which acted like an architect running his own practice, though of course under the general supervision of the men at the top.

An architect to whom a building was allocated could put his own ideas into its design without thinking that they would probably be removed at a later stage because his seniors had different ideas. He could regard it as a personal task and take a pride in achieving something with it. Working in a small unit, he no longer felt that he was only a minor cog in such a vast machine that his contribution was of no account.

This change in the work structure, together with other procedural changes that were introduced at the same time, did more than improve the quality of LCC architecture; it transformed the

C

whole spirit in which public authority work was approached, lifting it at once far above the level of bureaucratic routine. The same new spirit spread to other public offices, especially those of other local authorities—that is, the architect's departments of county councils and county boroughs—on whom the post-war building programmes had imposed a vast quantity of work.

The speed and completeness with which different offices adopted this new approach varied, of course, with the enlightenment or otherwise of the men at the top and the backing they were given by their elected councils and committees. Some retain to this day the old hierarchical pattern, which is reflected in the dreariness of their architecture, and not one has altogether overcome the difficulty of reconciling a creative occupation like architecture with the largely administrative preoccupations of the local government machine. For example no way has yet been found of dealing with the problem (which also exists, though to a lesser degree, in private offices) that the architect who rises to the top because of his ability tends to find himself in a position where he is chiefly an administrator and where the talents as a designer that got him there are no longer made use of.

The public architectural offices have thus to a great extent discarded their old image. This is not however solely due to the far-sighted policies adopted by a few heads of department, as at the London County Council. The opportunity was open to these because of the new importance accorded at the end of the war to the architectural role of public authorities. The state was increasingly taking responsibility for housing, school building and urban development generally, and the building programme in all these fields was enormous, owing to the new social and educational standards that were being aimed at and the shortage of accommodation caused by war-time destruction and the cessation of civil building during the war. The burden fell on the local authorities and their architects' departments, and architects generally, in the post-war climate of opinion, were conscious of the challenge made to them and the chance it offered of getting architecture recognised once more as a necessary social service.

There was thus a feeling in the air that the worthwhile opportunities were to be found not in private practice but in the public offices, and the ambitious young architects who had earlier despised this side of their profession now flocked there. It was to their advantage to do so, because a relatively junior architect entering a busy county or borough council office could expect to be put in charge of work of an importance that he would only rise to after years in private practice. Moreover, it was not only idealism that led so many young architects to join the public offices; another influence was the post-war restrictions on capital expenditure on building, controlled by a system of licences, which limited the activities of private architects and drove the newcomers into the public service as the available source of employment.

This is all old history, and the position is no longer the same today because, when the restrictions were lifted and more work came into the offices of private architects, many of those who had been eager to avail themselves of the opportunities offered by the public service, but had experienced some of its frustrations, remembered the delights of independence and left it to set up on their own. Nevertheless, the sudden rise to prominence of the public offices after the last war is of great importance because the architectural profession, as a result of it, will never be the same again. In spite of the continued appeal of private practice (fostered, as I have already observed, by the teaching methods in the architectural schools), architecture is now a respected branch of the public service, and in fact much of the solid work of the profession, and especially that share of it that does most to improve living standards, is done in the public or municipal offices, and the superior status that snobbery once allocated to fee-earning private practice no longer exists. It could perhaps be said that the significance and status of public practice was first recognised in 1946 when the city architect of Liverpool, Sir Lancelot Keay, became the first public authority architect to be elected president of the RIBA.

The various grades of public office offer an outlet for the architect's ingrained idealism, allowing him to collaborate closely with other officials similarly concerned with social betterment. Many of the advances, for example, that have been made in housing, education and welfare are due to the day-to-day alliance of the policy-makers in local government with the architects who translate housing and educational policy into flats and houses and old peoples' homes and schools.

Architects' direct involvement in the public service has also had a beneficial effect on architecture itself. Official architecture is by its nature impersonal and anonymous, and the large amount of work for which the public offices, as described above, are nowadays responsible provides the mass of straightforward unpretentious buildings badly needed in our towns and cities to offset the more individualistic buildings of the private architect—each competing with its neighbour—that have done so much to destroy their unity and harmony.

This impersonal public authority architecture is often dull and insensitive, but the fact that it does not shout out loud is a virtue in itself. There are some private architects who are content in the same way to regard their buildings as a contribution—even a humble contribution—to the general fabric of towns and cities, but there are too many who, perhaps encouraged by their clients' wish for self-advertisement, strive to be different and insist on trying to assert their own personalities in everything they design, an ambition legitimate enough in the occasional civic building, cathedral or public monument but quite out of place in, say, a block of offices or flats, a hotel or department store, which should be capable of settling into the existing townscape. The harm done to the environment by the lack of humility shown by many architects would be far greater if it was not for the routine contributions of the public offices.

The architect entering the public service has thus to forego the satisfaction of expressing his own personality through his buildings, though this need not prevent his becoming one of the leading figures in the profession, as several have already done. Several, too, have served for some years in the public service, risen to the top and then set up as private architects, a practice which has the advantage of creating a flow of private architects who have had experience of working closely with the various departments of local government and of the role of architecture as a social service.

There is not, in any case, a sharp division between the architects working in one of the public offices and those practising privately, because nearly all public authorities commission buildings from private architects as well as maintaining their own architects' departments. They are, in fact, among the most influential patrons of architecture. A large proportion of the work done by some private architects comes to them in this way and they too, therefore, get the benefit of working closely with the policy-making side of local government. Quite distinct from these—and for the most part, unfortunately, with a far lower standard both of design and of civic responsibility—are the large commercial offices working almost wholly for speculative and other property developers.

There are nowadays, in addition, numerous offices that have some of the characteristics of the public authority architect's department, since their work is impersonal and serves needs more like those of local authorities than those of the private or commercial client. For example the Coal Board, the Central Electricity Generating Board, British Rail and the national airlines all have their own architects' departments. So do the various hospital boards and the corporations responsible for the new towns. And in a similar category are banks, insurance companies and property developers, hotel owners and industrial companies, who also have staff architects serving their specialised needs. Some speculative builders, too, employ teams of architects to lay out and design housing estates. Much of the housing in the private sector is designed, however, without any architectural help, or only with the help of poorly qualified architectural assistants acting as little more than draughtsmen; hence the contrast in quality between the typical speculative builder's housing and the more skilful and responsibly designed council housing. Some building contractors employ qualified architects on their staffs, and they are liable to find themselves in an equivocal position since they can hardly be expected—as an architect should—to put the client's or the public's interest before the financial interest of the builder, if the builder is also their employer.

There is thus a great variety of employment available to the architect seeking an office to work in that will suit his particular interests and qualifications. Architects working for a salary in one kind of office or another, rather than on their own, are now a majority, and in spite of the rise of the public office, which seemed likely at one time to divide the profession into private and public sectors, the division today is into employer and employed. The rival claims of these two classes to dominate architecture's professional institutions is something I must discuss later. The big change since a couple of generations ago is that salaried employment is now a career in itself. Then, more often than not, the assistant in an architect's office, if himself a qualified architect, was simply passing through one of the stages on the way to independent practice. If he did not eventually emerge as an architect in his own right he was thought a failure.

Today the size of many offices—and especially the public ones—may mean that only a small minority of architects work as their own masters; but the subdivision of the large offices, private as well as public, into groups or teams—as I described earlier in this chapter when referring to the highly significant change of work structure pioneered in the London County Council around 1950—allows the leaders of these teams almost as much initiative and responsibility as independent architects. The group leader or job architect, or the partner or associate in a large private practice, is in effect the architect in charge of whatever building has been allocated to him, and he sees it through from beginning to end with only remote control from the chief architect (who is responsible to the council and its committees) in the case of a local authority office, and in the case of a private office after initial design conferences with the other partners. So all the satisfactions of creating buildings and seeing them constructed and brought into use are open to him, if not the satisfaction of having his name attached to them.

The other members of his team may be younger architects still working their way up, gaining experience (and sometimes moving from office to office to gain the widest possible experience) before themselves becoming partners or team-leaders; or they may be more senior architects not aiming to become independent—for there are many whom it does not suit to assume administrative responsibility, for whom working full-time at architecture is more important than being a leader and making a name. Some of these, the senior ones especially, have, as I have just made clear, responsible positions requiring all the qualities of an independent architect, but many more are employed mainly as draughtsmen, working on the enormous number of drawings required for all but the very simplest buildings, the preparation of which occupies a large proportion of the man-hours worked in an architect's office.

These drawings embody designs and decisions with which the draughtsman is not concerned, and this raises a question that has been discussed for a long time in the profession without a clear-cut answer being found: is it necessary for so many of the assistants who do this draughting work to be themselves qualified architects? It was stated earlier that as many as 70 per cent of architects are in salaried employment. This figure refers to fully qualified architects, and it is reasonable to ask whether it is not wasteful for so many young men (or women) to acquire the full range of qualifications an architect must have in order to do a job that needs only some of them. As long as all the necessary knowledge and expertise is available somewhere in the team, it can serve no purpose, the argument runs, for each member to possess all of it.

The present position, it can be claimed, is a relic of the time when every assistant was presumed to be on his way to himself becoming an architect, and of the now outdated pupilage system (see Chapter 6). But where will the permanent assistants or draughtsmen that the large office requires come from if it is no longer to be staffed by a moving population of the young on their way up and out? Is there not room for another type of assistant—for a separate category of architectural technicians, which is how they are best described—equipped with all the training necessary to a permanent assistant or draughtsman but not the full architect's qualifications, which a draughtsman will never use?

There are already, it is true, unqualified assistants in some offices, in addition to students working in the office while studying for their examinations, but these have no recognised status, are few in number and have not had a special technician's training.

There are, however, several objections to a separate category of architectural technicians. One is that it might introduce an undesirable class distinction into the profession—between the junior officer, as it were, and the permanent ranker—and destroy the unity that comes at present from everyone in an architect's office, apart from secretaries, filing clerks, telephonists and the like, sharing the same values and being involved in the same way in the standard of architecture ultimately achieved. A second objection concerns the client, who might feel less confidence in the service he could expect. At present he knows that he is dealing only with qualfied architects, though with less experienced ones at the lower levels, and he might be concerned at having to distinguish between a junior architect and an only partly qualified technician. A third objection is that the existence of certain members of the profession trained to fulfil only a limited role might reduce its flexibility. As things are at present, architects serving for the time being as draughtsmen can, because of their qualifications, move more easily from office to office, or even in or out of the public service, according to the load of work in different offices at any given time.

Finally, without a spell of service as a draughtsman, how would the young architect gain the experience he needs before he can take on fuller responsibilities? A draughtsman's work provides an essential grounding, especially because work at the drawing-board is not limited to turning out the routine working drawings required for the construction of a building, on which the full-time draughtsmen are engaged. Designing is done at the drawing-board too, and the architect who loses the habit of regarding himself as to some extent a draughtsman does so at his peril.

Yet in spite of the arguments outlined above, unless some drastic change takes place in office procedure (such as a change in the relationship between architect and building contractor, a vastly greater dependence on prefabricated building components or some new way of conveying information arising from com-puterisation), a change resulting in a marked reduction in the number of drawings an architect's office has to produce, the argument for a separate technician class will remain. The draughts-man or technician in Britain at least has the advantage of being closely integrated into the office in which he is employed. His situation can be contrasted with that of his equivalent in France, where he is more likely to work in a separate *bureau d'études* which produces the working drawings and details from the architect's sketches. The loser from this arrangement is the architect himself who easily becomes divorced from practical realities.

In Britain all kinds of office, whether private or public, follow the same methods of work and are responsible for the same tasks, in spite of the far-reaching changes, affecting architecture as a social service, that have been brought about by the growth of the public office. But there is one more problem arising therefrom that must be discussed in this chapter: the problem, for the architect, of maintaining a close enough relationship with the users of his buildings, who are not necessarily any longer the same as the clients who commission them.

In fact only in the case of a house commissioned by a private client has the architect ever found himself working personally for the future occupant of a building, and thus in a position to discover his needs by a direct process of question and answer, to analyse them with the future occupant's help and to consult with him at all stages of the design. In other cases where the architect is dealing with an individual client—say with the owner of a factory or of a business for which he is designing offices—he can similarly obtain all the information he wants, and although he may not be personally in touch with the factory or office workers, he will know enough about what they do and how they do it to be able to provide a convenient layout and appropriate working conditions.

Things are different, however, when he is working on one of the many types of building that the social services require, either as a member of a public authority architect's department or as a private architect commissioned by a public authority. In such cases access to the ultimate user's needs is far more difficult, and so therefore is the architect's task in meeting them. For one thing the actual users may not yet be known. A new school is sited and planned long before the particular children who will be taught in it are identifiable and in most cases before the teachers (whose views on accommodation and facilities would be invaluable) have been appointed. In a new hospital, patients, nurses, and domestic and medical staff will not yet be available to answer the architect's questions, though he may have access to some of the doctors (who will probably give him contradictory advice based on their experience in different circumstances). In the case of a housing scheme, layouts and accommodation have to be planned long before it is known who is going to live in the houses.

Architects also need access to the users of their buildings after they are finished and occupied, so that they can find out how well they work in practice and use this information to do better next time. There should be regular examination, and criticism, of buildings after some years of use. In the absence of this, most of the awards and prizes given, by government departments, the RIBA and other bodies, to meritorious new buildings are given on the basis of appearance rather than performance. The judges who have made some of these awards would have a shock if they revisited the buildings a few years afterwards.

Another problem typical of today is that the architect seldom has access, as it were, to the people on the spot. His source of information—in effect, the client who gives him his instructions—is a committee. It may be a committee of an educational authority, a regional hospital board, a housing authority or a new town corporation, and it may have specialist advice from the authority's technical officers; but like all committees it is unlikely to have a mind of its own, and may be concerned more with the political and financial aspects of its responsibilities—short-term aspects in most cases—than with the long-term values that such a lasting art as architecture must be based on.

The committee system is an essential part of democratic government, and there is no doubt that the very large part of the total building programme now—in Britain at least—under public control, and in practice controlled by committees of one kind or another, is as a result better related to social priorities. Building of this kind also makes a less disturbing impact on the environment, as we can see if we look around us, than the competitive free-for-all of private enterprise. Yet a sense of social responsibility does not of itself ensure good architecture, and the frustrations felt by many architects working for public authorities are only partly due to tedious bureaucratic procedures—to the fact that a committee tends to stifle the creative process. Their frustrations are also due to the difficulty of establishing a relationship with the actual users of buildings, without which architects cannot put their technical skills fully at society's disposal; nor can they make use of the ability, for which their training fits them, to foresee new solutions to existing problems. For the architect has a wider role than that of designer of buildings.

CHAPTER THREE

The Professional Man

The architect's basic professional role is to fulfil the demands his clients make on him efficiently and agreeably, but he also has a wider role, of two kinds. The first, which is to do his share of controlling and improving the total environment, I have already touched on; the second is to help ensure that the kind of demands made on him are those that will allow him to work to his maximum capacity. For besides giving people what they already want in the way of buildings and the settings buildings occupy, he is also the person best qualified to show them what they could have if they chose to demand something better.

This aspect of his work has become far more significant since the elected bodies that make up our democratic society became, as described in the preceding chapter, the largest patrons of architecture; but showing what architecture is capable of doing for his private clients is also part of the architect's duty. Democracy suggests that the architect should give the public what it wants, but what the public wants is only what it is accustomed to, unless proof can be offered to it that something better could be made available if the demand were there; and in the case of buildings—the standards of comfort and accommodation they set and the style of the life they provide for—the man to show the public what it could have if it asked for it is the architect.

Complaints to speculative builders about vulgar and illiterate standards of design in new housing estates almost invariably elicit the answer: that is what people want. But they would want something better if they knew about it—not necessarily at once, but after a process of enlightenment in which architects and their representative institutions should take a lead, both by example and, for instance, by encouraging more attention to architecture and the environment in schools, where they are now almost ignored. Those British suburban estates which are noticeably better designed (such as those promoted by the now defunct Span company and by a few other conscientious developers) are better simply because an architect (in the case of Span, Mr Eric Lyons) exercised the opportunity of leadership open to architects and showed what the alternatives were. The influence of this company's housing projects has been enormous.

This does not mean that everyone should be expected to conform to architects' tastes. They are trained to appreciate order, and the qualities that therefore appeal to them include reticence and regularity (which explains why so many architects live in Georgian houses), with results that others might consider dull. But a good architect is capable of designing for others besides himself. He should remember that some of the qualities liked by the less sophisticated public, which he may think vulgar, serve a useful purpose as well as giving pleasure. They provide reassurance and a sense of stability and status, which people who can afford it achieve for themselves by living in something old, whose historic styles provide their own kind of status. There can be a place for make-believe in architecture, the main thing against it being that it devalues what it imitates.

However, the psychology of taste is outside the scope of this book. What matters, in the present context of the architect's obligations, is that people should have the maximum choice, and certainly not be made to feel they must accept whatever is given them. Whether the architect is explaining to a business man the benefit he can expect from some alternative to the usual layout of an office block, or whether he is explaining to a housing authority the advantages, in terms of comfortable living as well as the economical use of land, of some alternative to the conventional semi-detached villas strung out along a traffic road, he is enlarging the scope both of architecture's social usefulness and of his own opportunities.

Intent though he may be, however, on fulfilling his obligations to architecture and the environment, the private architect—though not the public authority architect—is handicapped by the uncertain ways in which jobs come to him. This is not new. It has long been his complaint that the best architects are not necessarily those most in demand and that there is no recognised way of putting people in need of an architect's services in touch with the most suitable practitioner. Chance contacts are relied on, and this is made the more unsatisfactory by most people's remarkable ignorance of just what an architect does and where his responsibilities begin and end. Everyone knows why he goes to a doctor, but few know why and when an architect is required, what sort of relationship is to be expected between client and architect and what their mutual obligations are. The result is that choosing an architect presents difficulties simply of communication, and is complicated by several misconceptions; for example by the notion that if an architect is well known or well established he will charge higher fees, whereas in fact fees, in Britain at least, are (with certain exceptions—see Chapter 5) the same for all architects and follow a scale fixed by the Royal Institute of British Architects and based on the cost of the work to be done.

Perhaps the best reason for employing a particular architect is that a previous building of his is liked or recommended. It is satisfactory to the architect to know that he has been chosen on merit, and if a client likes an architect's work and stays with him, a relationship can be built up, of trust and understanding, that will make life easier for both and is likely to result in better buildings. But many clients build only once and may not have the opportunity or the inclination to examine other buildings of a similar kind, or the knowledge to deduce which of the qualities they like or dislike in a particular building are attributable to the architect.

A client with no experience of building may choose an architect recommended to him by someone who knows his work, and this is at least more satisfactory than a choice not based on architectural merit at all. It used to be said that the first thing an ambitious young architect should do is to join a golf club or find other ways of making social contacts with businessmen whose acquaintance might be useful. The business world, fortunately, does not now put so much reliance on social connections, but it is still remarkable how many architects are appointed without knowledge of their qualification for a particular job; for example because they are related to, or socially known to, directors of companies or members of committees or their friends. Standards of architecture will not begin to improve until decisions of this kind are made more sensibly and logically. There are too many second-rate architects and they continue to exist because ignorant businessmen and others continue to employ them.

Architects are employed, too, for other reasons not connected with their ability to design good buildings. The deplorable architectural standard of the office blocks and similar buildings with which property developers have disfigured our cities in recent years is simply explained by the fact that they are nearly all designed by a limited number of second-rate architects who are in command of prosperous practices solely concerned with property development. Such architects are employed by property companies, and by the big insurance companies responsible for investment in property, because of their knowledge and experience of the financial aspects of site development. They advise on the financial possibilities of particular sites and on how to exploit them and overcome the restrictions the various town-planning regulations place on their profitability. They may even find their clients promising sites ripe for redevelopment, though this brings them close to the kind of involvement in business operations from which they are supposed to be debarred by their professional status.

For such architects, as for their clients, a building is only so much lettable floor-space, and it is not surprising that the results are disastrous. The blame for the damage they inflict on cities must, however, rest on the clients as well as on this minority of commercially orientated and aesthetically uneducated architects. A high standard of building depends on clients interested in architecture and proud of the buildings for which they are responsible. Unfortunately there is no longer a tradition, as there was a century or two ago, of the building promoter taking pride in his position as a patron of architecture. The men of power are no longer the men of taste.

We cannot expect a return to the past. Power is nowadays differently exercised—often, as I have already remarked, through boards and committees instead of by individuals. But some knowledge and understanding of architecture on the part of those responsible for new buildings in our towns and cities is urgently required, the only alternative being even stricter official control of their activities. This is not altogether desirable since it would also place restrictions on experimental and more imaginative architecture and might, in any case, not be effectively exercised since the controlling officials themselves, and more especially the elected committees to whom, in our democratic society, the officials are responsible, may not be any more discriminating about architecture than the businessmen, even though they may not regard building solely as a source of profit. Solid improvement will not happen until some interest in, and understanding of, architecture comes once more to be regarded as part of an educated man's equipment. The starting place for such an improvement must therefore be the schools and school teachers.

In the meantime it would help if businessmen realised—and this is something the better architects can demonstrate to them—that buildings designed by really good architects are economical and provide better working conditions, and are therefore good for business; and especially that a distinguished building is a good advertisement. All these things have long been appreciated in America—hence the far higher standard of big-city architecture. A few recent London office buildings, designed to be occupied by the companies that built them, not as speculations, show that this is beginning to be understood in Britain too.

So the choice of a suitable architect is the beginning of good architecture. In Britain the main professional institution is sometimes able to play a useful part in helping potential clients to choose the right architect. The president of the Royal Institute of British Architects keeps lists of architects experienced in various types of building, and is accustomed to recommend names for a client to follow up. His choice is sometimes rather conservative but is always honest (though there were stories a generation or so ago of presidents recommending themselves) and it is to be relied on because he has to think of the good name of the profession.

The oldest established method of finding an architect for an important building is, unfortunately, not as often used as in the past. This is the competition. In the nineteenth century nearly all public buildings were the subject of an architectural competition, and this is still so in some countries, notably Scandinavia. But the practice has declined in Britain and America. It had its drawbacks without doubt. But it also offered considerable advantages, and should be more often resorted to, especially now that forms of competition have been devised which enable the main drawback to be overcome.

This drawback is the waste of effort involved when a large number of architects—sometimes a couple of hundred in a popular competition—all work on designs only one of which is going to be built, the number of man-hours required to produce the necessary drawings being enormous. This waste of effort can be reduced by the two-stage competition, in which architects are expected only to submit rough sketches and not whole sets of finished drawings. On the basis of these sketches a few architects are chosen to work their designs out fully before a final judgement is made. The client still gains the advantage of having a large number of trained minds focused on his particular problem, thus multiplying by that number the chances of finding the ideal solution. In a two-stage competition it is usual to pay each architect chosen for the second stage a fee to cover his expenses. In an open competition, in which no such fees are paid, there are much larger prizes for the winners and runners-up (in an important competition perhaps £5,000 for the winner and £3,000 and £2,000 for those adjudged second and third), but this is not as costly to the client as it sounds because the first prize is counted as a first instalment of the fees the winning architect will eventually get.

What he is competing for is therefore not the cash prize but the appointment as architect of a building. In theory it would be possible for a clever architect to make a living by repeatedly winning the second or third prizes in competitions without doing any building at all, but this would hardly satisfy the ambitions of a true architect, who finds fulfilment in the fact of building.

Another form of competition favoured in recent years, also less wasteful than the open competition, is the limited competition in which perhaps half a dozen architects, known to be well qualified for the particular job required, are invited to submit ideas (again being paid a fee) and the architect is selected from these.

This is an efficient and economical form of competition but it discards the main advantage of the competition system, that of disclosing unknown talent. In the nineteenth century many famous architects first made their name by winning competitions, and young architects starting in practice but with not enough work to keep them busy have always filled in time entering competitions, on the chance of suddenly acquiring a commission of a size and importance they could not expect to acquire by other means. Competitions are therefore important to the profession as a means of getting young architects a start, and the more so while the procedure for obtaining work remains as haphazard as I have already shown it to be. There is no need for the prospective client who utilises the competition system to be afraid of being landed with too inexperienced an architect, because there is always a clause in the conditions that allows the assessor (the judge who decides the winners) to give first prize to an insufficiently experienced architect on the understanding that he goes into partnership with someone more experienced for the purpose of executing his design.

Much depends, of course, on the judging of competitions. This used to be done by a solitary assessor, an eminent architect whose tastes and prejudices competitors used to study carefully in order to produce a design with the best possible chance of appealing to him. Nowadays a group of assessors is more usual—say three architects. A larger number might put out of the running architects who ought to be free to compete, because in spite of what I have said about the usefulness of the competition system in giving chances to young architects, many established architects compete as well. They do so for the obvious reason that they would like the job, but also as a way of keeping the assistants in their office busy when times are slack. It is one of the perpetual problems of private practice that the pressure of work is very uneven—an architect is unusually fortunate if a new job comes along just when another is finishing—yet a team of assistants used to working with each other and accustomed to the architect's and his partners' ways is a valuable asset. Architectural firms are reluctant to disperse such a team when a job comes to an end, knowing they will be unable to reassemble it when another job starts. The gap can usefully (and with luck profitably) be filled by setting underemployed staff to work on competition drawings. In fact it has its profitable side, win or lose, since the studies involved in preparing a competition design are themselves profoundly educational.

Sometimes the assessors appointed to judge a competition include one or more non-architects; for example a representative of the client, or someone with expert knowledge if the subject is a building serving some specialised purpose—perhaps a scientist if it is a building for scientific research. This extra help should not however be necessary if the competition brief (that is, the written description of what is required) has been properly prepared. The brief is the responsibility of the assessors in consultation with the clients, and once it has been incorporated in the competition conditions it is better that the judging should be done only by architects, who are used to reading and interpreting drawings and have a common analytical method.

If there are non-architects on a panel of assessors it is one of the RIBA rules that architects must be in a majority. The conduct of architectural competitions is governed by strict rules laid down by the RIBA, and members of the institute are not allowed to take part in any competition not organised according to these rules and of which the RIBA has not approved the conditions. This is necessary to ensure fairness and avoid abuse of the system, but has caused difficulties since British architects began to enter comtitions held in other countries, where sometimes competitions are not so strictly run or fairly judged. However, as a result of recent efforts by the International Union of Architects, there are more international competitions with rules the RIBA has no need to disapprove, and more participation by British architects—a change to be welcomed in view of Britain's membership of the European Economic Community.

The RIBA's rules for the conduct of competitions cover conditions of entry, the process of judging and what happens afterwards. The number, size and style of drawings must be laid down, so that fanciful or elaborate presentation gains no advantage. Judging must be anonymous. Competitors send in their drawings unsigned but with a sealed envelope containing their names. A number is then placed on each set of drawings and on the envelope, and only after the assessors have finished judging and have awarded the prizes are the envelopes opened and the authorship of the winning designs disclosed. Designs have to be accompanied by estimates of cost, and the assessors, usually with the help of a quantity surveyor, have to satisfy themselves that the design could in fact be built for the amount stated; if not it is ineligible for a prize. Designs are also ineligible, of course, if they do not meet the other conditions or if their authors try to make their identity known or otherwise influence the judging, and when the competition is over there are rules about publicly exhibiting the entries so that the competition is not only fair but can be seen to be fair.

Finally—one of the most important rules of all—the winner of the competition must be appointed architect for the building if and when it goes ahead. No one can be compelled to put up a building if he chooses not to, but it is reasonable to ask him to undertake, if he is to have the advantage of a number of architects making designs to suit his needs, that the architect fairly judged the winner should be given the job.

The conduct of competitions is only one among many tasks undertaken by the Royal Institute of British Architects, and this may be a good place to introduce the institute and describe its relationship to the profession. It is in effect the British profession's governing body, though contrary to common belief an architect is not obliged to be a member. Since the Architects' Registration Act was passed in 1931, the word 'architect' has been protected; that is, no one may describe himself as an architect unless his name is on the official register of architects—though in Britain this does not prevent him from designing buildings. This register of architects is maintained not by the RIBA but by a statutory body, set up in 1938 under a subsequent Act, called the Architects' Registration Council, so that a man (or woman) may be a registered architect, and entitled to practise as such, without being a member of the RIBA. If he *is* a member, he can call himself a 'chartered architect', since the RIBA has a Royal Charter, a distinction conferred on a professional body if it satisfies the Privy Council that its organisation and regulations are in the public interest.

It is the RIBA which sets the standard for entry to the profession by supervising the work of the architectural schools and holding its own examinations (which are in fact the only ones recognised by the Architects' Registration Council). Because of this, and because it was organising and representing architects for nearly a hundred years before the Registration Council was set up by the Act, the RIBA is accepted as the ruling body. To the public in general, membership of the RIBA is synonymous with being an architect. The institute, in practice, represents and controls the profession in Britain in nearly every way, and most architects (roughly 85 per cent) do belong. In addition, many architects in the Commonwealth countries belong also, a practice that dates from the time when these countries possessed neither architects' institutes nor architectural schools of their own; when the only professional rules they conformed to were the British rules and most Commonwealth students came to Britain for their training.

Today architects' institutes exist in most countries, though their form differs widely and so does the strictness of the control they exercise. In America the national controlling body is the American Institute of Architects, but only just over half the qualified architects in the country belong and licences to practise are granted, not by the institute, but by Boards of Architectural Registration in the different states; so that an architect can practise only in the state where he is registered unless he obtains separate registration from another state's board and perhaps takes another examination.

The Royal Institute of British Architects began as a learned society, established, as defined in its first Royal Charter of 1837, for 'the general advancement of Civil Architecture and for promoting and facilitating the acquirement of the knowledge of the various Arts and Sciences connected therewith'. These are still its purposes, though during nearly a century and a half it has acquired numerous responsibilities, political, social and technical, which make it a good deal more than a learned society. It still, however, runs one of the most complete architectural libraries in the world, with over 80,000 volumes, and a monthly journal.

I have already mentioned its work in supervising architectural education, which I shall return to in a later chapter, its control of the fees architects may charge and of architectural competitions and its code of professional conduct, designed to ensure that clients employing a member can rely on disinterested advice. This code states that he may not seek to take work away from other architects and that he may not cut fees—that is, offer to do work for a smaller fee than is laid down by the official scale, which fixes the fees he should charge for different kinds of work. He may not be a director of a company with a business in any way related to architecture, such as a contracting firm or a firm manufacturing building materials. He may not accept a commission from a contractor or tradesman. He may not advertise, although while a building is under construction he may put up a notice (in a standard form, with letters not more than 2in high) stating that he is the architect.

The RIBA also runs a Professional Services Board to give advice and guidance to its members—not, however, about their architecture but about their relations with clients and with the building industry. The standard form of building contract (referred to, however, by the judge during a law case in October 1972 as 'a farrago of obscurities'), was drawn up by the RIBA, and it conducts arbitrations when there is a dispute. It also serves as the profession's spokesman by putting the architect's point of view to the government, to industry and elsewhere, and organises propaganda on behalf of architects and to promote public understanding of architecture.

Leaving aside student members, not yet qualified, the institute has about 19,000 members of whom roughly 50 per cent are in private practice. Half of these are principals or partners and the other half salaried assistants. Another 40 per cent of the total are employed in the public service and the remaining 10 per cent are engaged in teaching or research or writing (like the author of this book) or have jobs in industry. Three-quarters of all the members are thus in salaried employment—a proportion that has grown enormously in the past twenty-five years—and the RIBA has been criticised recently, as I have already noted, for preserving too much of its original character, that of an organisation designed to serve and protect the private architect.

How far it should move towards being a trade union rather than a learned society is, in view of its duty to architecture as well as to architects, a matter for debate, but after an internal upheaval in 1972, arising partly from the discontent of its salaried members and partly from a financial crisis, there is now a somewhat stronger representation of salaried architects on its council, though not as strong as the most extreme reformers would like.

The financial crisis was due to a large extent to the problems common, in these days of sharply rising costs, to all organisations with a limited income, and they could have been solved, at least temporarily, by increasing subscriptions. This was proposed, but was resented by the majority of salaried members who thought that too much money was being spent on activities of no immediate benefit to themselves, and some of these activities have for the time being been curtailed. It was certainly true that the RIBA had expanded into an ambitious bureaucratic organisation concerning itself with long-term investigations into matters like office management and the classification of technical information, which were undoubtedly useful but not immediately helpful to the mass of the membership, and that it had expanded at the same time by opening branch offices in various centres outside London—a move designed to benefit all members, but again only in the long run. And it may be that it had stretched its activities beyond those proper to a professional institute.

The rights and wrongs of these and similar controversies are only important because they illustrate the dilemma facing any body like the RIBA. It has to decide where the priorities lie, and it could be argued that the RIBA has either failed to decide or has got them wrong. But it has not, it seems to me, been wrong in looking after the interests of one sector of the membership rather than another, so much as wrong in being on the side of architects as they are, rather than as they should be. If this is so, the rebellious element has been trying to push the institute in an irrelevant direction.

The dilemma I have just referred to arises from the fact that since the RIBA consists, fundamentally, of the bulk of its members, since they all pay a subscription and have the right to elect the council, it tends to behave as though it had an equal duty to all of them. Yet this conflicts with the RIBA's duty to advance the art of architecture, enjoined in its charter. It cannot be denied— though the RIBA by implication denies it by treating all its members equally—that there are too many poor-quality architects. We have only to look around our towns and cities to see that this is so. There is too much second-rate work done by RIBA members, and the institute's first priority should be to improve the quality of its membership.

This will mean raising the standard of entry to the profession, which the RIBA is in a position to do since it supervises the curricula of the architectural schools and their qualifying examinations. Until this has had the desired result it will mean endeavouring to direct work to the better architects so as to minimise the harm done by the worse architects—in spite of the latter being also members of the RIBA. It will mean accepting criticism of architects' work and acting on it, and even itself initiating criticism, which will not be popular since it will be criticising its own members, who may claim to be immune since they have paid their subscriptions.

I am not referring to members who transgress the RIBA code of conduct by improper commercial dealings, by cutting fees or by other unprofessional practices. There are bound to be a few of these, as there are bound to be black sheep in any profession. Such transgressors are already dealt with, though perhaps not as promptly or as publicly as they should be, and they chiefly matter when they bring architecture itself into disrepute. I am referring to architects who are simply not good enough at their job and are incapable, in particular, of improving through their work the quality of the environment society has to put up with—

or are unwilling to put themselves or their clients out in order to do so.

The RIBA has many other obligations, most of which it is already fulfilling conscientiously, but to raise standards so that anyone employing one of its members can be sure of getting skilful and responsible service should come first. If the RIBA does not undertake this reform no one else will. How urgently it is needed is shown by the way the public is already beginning to blame architects for the deterioration of the environment—as regards a good proportion of architects unjustly, but even a small minority can do harm that invalidates much of the good done by the majority. That the environment is being spoilt by other happenings, outside architects' control, gives architects as a profession no excuse for inaction. They must take the responsibility which is theirs and they can set, in addition, a useful lead.

Besides the town-planning controls discussed in the preceding chapter, which are operated by local authorities under the general supervision of the Ministry of the Environment, there is one other body concerned with protecting the environment—including protecting it against poor-quality or self-indulgent architecture. This is the Royal Fine Art Commission, an oddly named body since it has almost nothing to do with the fine arts. It, too, has been the subject of recent controversy. The commission was set up by Act of Parliament in 1922 to serve as a watch-dog on behalf of the public. It was originally intended to examine and comment on the designs for new public buildings, but later its powers were extended to allow it to comment on all buildings that affect public amenity (that is, the only designs it is not concerned with are those of privately owned buildings out of sight of the public and those of interiors of buildings). The commission does not have to wait to be consulted; it has been given by Parliament the right to call for any plans it wants to look at. Its interest is in the appearance of new buildings and their effect on their surroundings, not on their practical efficiency, and properly used it could be a useful instrument—not for creating better architects, which only the profession itself can do, but for minimising the harm done by poor ones and, equally important, for helping all architects and those who employ them to achieve a better relationship between buildings and their settings.

The commission's powers are limited because it can only give advice; it cannot insist on its advice being taken. This is right; to give such a body the power of veto over designs it did not like would be to institute a form of aesthetic censorship. It can nevertheless exercise a useful influence through the general guidance it gives and through the pronouncements it makes about projects that come before it (though it often fails to make such pronouncements, especially when they are critical, forcibly and promptly enough), and it can influence architects individually through the detailed and expert discussions it has with them. It can often have a decisive influence because many public bodies, including the planning committees of local authorities, use the commission as a kind of arbitrator, making the granting of planning permission in certain cases conditional on the Fine Art Commission's approval.

Its influence for good is weakened, unfortunately, by the failure of the government itself to give it support. Since the commission was set up by the government for the very purpose of giving advice about architecture, one would expect the government to treat it as its appointed adviser and take its advice unless there is some very good external reason for overruling it. In practice the government accords it no special standing, and often ignores its advice or fails to consult it, thus creating much frustration among its members. The commission is criticised by the public when things go wrong, though often it has been helpless to intervene.

Most of the recent controversy about the commission has however been on a different issue, and results from a difficult internal problem. The commission consists of a chairman and about fifteen members, appointed by the Prime Minister for a five-year term which is renewable, and unpaid. Half the members are architects, which even if it was not desirable is unavoidable because it is difficult to find others with enough understanding of architecture—or even, unfortunately, with enough interest—and with the ability to read architects' drawings. But architects have their own embarrassments when they have to pronounce judgements on each other's work, and there is even greater embarrassment when designs by architect-members of the commission are among those it has to deal with. They behave correctly, leaving the discussion to their colleagues. But justice should be seen to be done, and the involvement of architects in advising about what they and their colleagues do adds to the impression that punches are somehow being pulled.

The fault however does not lie with the architects but with the failure of educated people to take enough interest in architecture and become knowledgeable judges of it, with the result that a commission composed principally of non-architects could not be trusted to make sensible and well balanced judgements. Unless he trains his eyes and takes trouble to learn what architects are trying to do, everyone feels safe only with what is familiar, and it is one of the tragedies of today that people who show real appreciation, based on open-minded study of, say, modern poetry or modern music remain ignorant about modern architecture.

Like the architect himself, the Royal Fine Art Commission has been interesting itself increasingly in environmental problems. These include the siting of buildings and their effect on their surroundings, and also the kind of total environment a town or village offers, which involves not only its new buildings but those already existing. A town's old streets and buildings give it its essential character, to which new developments should be thoughtfully related, and the survival of old buildings permits its history to remain written on its face—a quality that helps it maintain its particular personality when the tendency of rebuilding is to make all places look more and more alike.

There has lately been much public concern about the destruction of old buildings, which has been reflected in government action and legislation, in obligations placed by the government on local authorities and in the attitudes to old buildings shown by architects—not only those who have chosen to specialise in the repair and restoration of old buildings, but by all architects, for a very large part of the work architects do in urban areas involves, if not the destruction of existing buildings, at least changes in their use and in the settings in which they find themselves. Architects are widely blamed for the disappearance of buildings, or even whole areas of towns, that people had become attached to. Sometimes they are justly blamed, sometimes unjustly; but at least architects can claim that it was members of their profession who led the campaign against indiscriminate destruction which has recently created new attitudes on the part of the government and the public.

The first success of this campaign was better protection for historic monuments, which are now listed, classified and legally safeguarded in many ways, though not so effectively as they might be if only because local authorities, who operate the safeguarding legislation, are often themselves careless of the fate of monuments in their area; also because the laws that forbid the demolition of a historic building do not prevent the owner from letting it deteriorate to the point where it falls down or has to be pulled down.

More recently it was realised that to preserve the individual monument (though this is vitally important because historic buildings are an essential part of our inheritance since one epoch passes its culture on to the next largely by the way it builds) does little to ensure that towns and cities retain the good qualities their architects have endowed them with over the centuries. Nearly always there are groups of buildings—whole streets or even larger areas—of which the individual buildings may not be remarkable enough to deserve preservation for their own sake, but which add up to something of quality and character, without which the place would be poorer. The latest legislation, especially the 1967 Civic Amenities Act, empowers and encourages local authorities to look after these areas better—areas on which the individuality of towns largely depends—by designating conservation areas within which special rules apply.

This is where the architects' co-operation is vital, because the objective is not that conservation areas should remain untouched; only that priority should be given to maintaining their existing character. Rebuilding has often to be done there, but it needs the humility too many architects lack and a careful attention to scale and materials, without however falling back on the easy solution of simply imitating the old, which would bring the whole process of cultural evolution to a stop. Weaving the new into the fabric of the old is a fascinating and rewarding exercise that provides a test for all an architect's skills—far more so than making a clean sweep of everything existing in the area as a preliminary to re-development, which architects used to think of as their right.

Architects sometimes feel impeded by this concern for what already exists and argue, justly, that past ages have not hesitated to demolish old buildings in order to put up new. It is true that preservationism can be overdone, and that some of those who campaign for everything old to be preserved are moved by a nostalgic preference for whatever represents the past and have no appreciation of modern architecture even when it is good of its kind. The remedy however lies in the architects' own hands. Excessive demands for the preservation of everything old are due not only to love of old buildings but to mistrust of what present-day architects are likely to put in their place. So the best answer to unreasonable preservationism is better quality architecture, less self-important and assertive and more sensitive to its surroundings.

Taking the long view, therefore, the architect's aim should be to strike a balance between conservation and renewal. On this being successfully done the future of our cities as civilised settings for our own lives increasingly depends. Architects are better equipped, by their training and experience, to make the judgements it requires and a sense of responsibility towards problems of this kind is one of the duties their profession owes to society.

CHAPTER FOUR

What Kind of Person?

The preceding chapters have dealt with the architect's duties and responsibilities, with the professional bodies through which he is organised and with his relationship generally to the society he serves; in fact with architects as a class. But what about the man himself? How different is he from other people who have chosen other occupations, and why did he choose this one?

First it should perhaps be made clear that, for the sake of simplicity and brevity, I have been using the word 'he' without meaning to imply that the architect cannot alternatively be a she. There are in fact a number of woman architects, but not nearly as many as there should be in a profession just as well suited to women as to men. No women have yet become eminent as architects, either through their work in private practice or by reaching the top in one of the public architectural offices.

It used to be objected that women could not be architects because they would have to climb ladders, though it was never explained whether this was because of what people standing beneath might see or because women were supposed to be in some way unsteady. Now that women wear trousers and have proved their athleticism in many sports, these objections need not be taken seriously. In any case, climbing ladders is a negligible part of an architect's activities. A more real handicap is the same one that relates to woman doctors and scientists: after marriage and child-rearing have compelled women temporarily to give up practice, it is not easy to return because they may find themselves out of touch with recent technical and other developments. But this should not be difficult to overcome in the case of architecture, especially in view of the prevalence of partnerships in modern practice.

In the nineteenth century, it is true, there was an assumption that all the professions were for men, but that was a long time ago, and the medical profession and a number of others have successfully overcome this kind of prejudice. Women now enter the architectural schools in good numbers; in fact they have been doing so for fully half a century. Although marriage or other distractions, in the present as in the past, prevent many from finishing the course, those that do so work as competently as men as assistants in offices—private and public—but they seldom get far beyond that stage. This is one of those mysteries that time may yet resolve.

Meanwhile (and again only for the sake of simplicity) I shall use the word 'man' throughout this book, and the reader must take it as meaning—unless the context indicates otherwise—'man or woman'. It must now be asked: what kind of individual, man or woman, becomes an architect? This question needs clarifying because people sometimes embark on an architectural career for reasons quite unrelated to the suitability of either their talents or their temperaments: for example because their father is an architect and there is therefore a ready-made practice for them to step into immediately on qualifying. So the question should take a more precise form: what kind of people choose to become architects because their ambitions and inclinations lead them in this direction, and what qualities are in fact required of an architect? I have deliberately not referred to the qualities required of a *successful* architect, since success—that is, commercial success —depends on many chance factors and on business acumen and opportunity, and the most deserving are not necessarily the most successful. If a good architect is not always successful, still less does it follow that all the successful architects are good ones.

The most necessary quality for a good architect is one that it is particularly difficult to gauge in advance: the ability to visualise things in three dimensions; to be able to estimate from two-dimensional drawings the effect of a building as a solid object and the way its form will change or appear to change from varying viewpoints. This, however, is a talent that has to be cultivated. So, to a great extent, are the other talents an architect needs; and to foster them, as well as to instil knowledge, is the purpose of the training at an architectural school.

Yet certain personality traits and predispositions indicate the likelihood of the right talents eventually emerging. It is a good beginning, for instance, if the prospective architect is positively interested in the appearance of things and observant about them, and has an instinctive sense of order; that is, if he minds about events as well as objects having a logical and comprehensible relation to each other, and forming a pattern rather than occurring haphazardly. These two traits together hold some promise of developing the qualities architects need in order to perform their two principal roles: that of selecting and discriminating in matters of the eye, and that of creating order out of chaos. The second of the two traits also promises practical efficiency. The architect spends a lot of his time being a businessman, and ought to be a capable one; for if he cannot make sure that a building is finished to time and within the estimate of cost, no amount of aesthetic endeavour will earn him a good reputation or save his profession from being called unreliable. Competence in running his own office is a test of his competence all round.

There are certain subjects which are supposed, if schoolboys are good at them, to indicate the suitability of architecture as a career, especially drawing and mathematics. Both are useful to the prospective architect, but more because a talent for them indicates the right potentialities than because it is essential in itself. An architect must indeed draw, since drawing is the means

E   65

of working out and recording ideas—it is an almost indispensable part of the process of designing—but not usually in the way a schoolboy has learnt to draw. It can in fact be argued that a facility for making effective sketches leads architects to deceive themselves into imagining that their buildings will necessarily possess the qualities they have illustrated in their drawings. Drawing in the quite different sense of producing the sheets of plans, sections, elevations and details which comprise the routine work of an architect's office can be learnt by almost anyone.

As to mathematics, a mathematical sense indicates an inclination towards system and logic, but architects can manage without advanced mathematics in these days of partnership with engineers and other aids to reliable calculation.

Young men and young women thus sometimes decide to become architects because the school subjects they are good at are those obviously related to the practice of architecture. But often the decision is taken for reasons more connected with the work an architect does than with the skills he needs. His work has an appeal because the end-product is something concrete and visible, responding to people's instinct for making things—an instinct that does not only find fulfilment in making them with the hands; or because it combines opportunities for self-expression with a sense of social service, the latter being implicit in architecture's identity as one of the professions.

The fact of its being classed as a profession may, on the other hand, appeal for snobbish reasons. An architect is a kind of gentleman, or so some parents find it reassuring to believe (though perhaps parents now have less say in a son's career than they used to do). It is true that the architect runs a business supplying certain services on demand, but he is thought to occupy a superior position to others in business or trade. What is more important to the young aspirant than to his status-minded parent is that if he has to be a businessman the architect has the opportunity to be an artist as well. In fact many good architects began with the creative and imaginative instincts associated with artists of every kind, and decided that it would suit them best to channel these instincts into a practical occupation like architecture. Alternatively, there are those who have begun with an interest in old buildings, from which it is only a logical step to taking an interest in carrying forward into the present the traditions old buildings represent and seeing how they respond to new circumstances. Any but the most superficial study of historic buildings involves acquiring some knowledge and understanding of their whys and wherefores and how they were put together, which means a basic understanding of architecture itself.

When young men or women have become architects, for one or other of these reasons—or, more likely, for a combination of several—or have just drifted into architecture for no reason they can analyse, and have then completed their course of training, what kind of people do they then turn out to be, and what kind of life do they find themselves living? The architect conforms no more strictly to a type than anyone else. I have already described him, in the opening paragraphs of this book, as a mixture of artist and businessman. Some architects lean towards the Bohemian characteristics, in life-style and appearance, of the traditional artist, while some are hardly distinguishable from other businessmen. Yet architects have many characteristics in common, arising from the interests that have led them to become architects and the life their work obliges them to lead; one notable characteristic being, for example, that their work is not a separate part of their daily life. Those in other professions may be able to set work aside when they leave the office at six o'clock and resume it next morning, but an architect spends nearly all his waking life being an architect. Not that he works all the time, but his leisure hours and holidays tends to be dominated by interests related to architecture. Inevitably, as he follows his daily routine, the streets he walks along and every building he enters or leaves in the course of it—his bank, a department store, a railway station or even a public lavatory—mean something different to him than they would to a lawyer or an accountant. His eyes are always open and he is professionally aware, consciously or subconsciously, of what they show him.

Still more is this true of his own house and those of his friends. The inside of his house, in particular, takes on to a great extent the nature of one of his own designs. It is not necessarily a conscious advertisement of his capacity and taste, and is seldom an elegant piece of interior design—an architect's family is no tidier or all of a pattern than anyone else's—but the objects in it are chosen where in other people's houses they may simply be accumulated. Colours, too, are imposed rather than allowed to happen and there is a sense of the interior being looked at as a whole; he may have altered the levels and spaces, for example by throwing rooms together in a bolder fashion than others would embark on, and he may have built in a lot of the furniture.

He may indeed have built the house himself. Most architects during the course of their lives build—or at least convert—a house for their own occupation. They naturally have an urge to put their ideas into practice without at the same time having to satisfy the needs, or obey the whims, of someone else. For a young architect building his own house provides invaluable experience, but he does not generally stay in it for long, not only for the usual reason of change of circumstances or a growing family, but because of a feeling that he himself has outgrown the particular stage in his development as a designer that the house represents.

Architects are fastidious critics of their own work, but they like praise from their colleagues; so much so that it is said with some justice that they have the habit of looking only to each other for approbation. Their habit of critical analysis makes them restive as occupants of houses designed by themselves, and it is common for architects, when they can afford it, to build or convert for their use a succession of houses, moving on simply because of the urge to build anew as their ideas evolve, or perhaps because of the appeal of a site they have discovered whose potentialities they feel only they can realise.

Architects are naturally discriminating about the houses they inhabit when not designed by themselves (I have already referred to the attraction Georgian houses have for them, on account of their geometrical purity and rational layout); they are also discriminating about the locality, being aware of environment as something that can be influenced instead of being allowed to happen. This explains the number of architects who are to be found living in areas with a designed and positive character (in London, Holland Park and Islington and Hampstead Garden Suburb) or in consciously planned environments like New Ash Green in Kent. Being individualists, however, they are less willing than they ought to be to give time and energy to working for the improvement of the local environment, by serving on parish and district councils. They join local amenity societies and local branches of professional organisations, but the pressure that bodies like this can exercise comes from without, which architects appear perversely to prefer, whereas their influence inside decision-making bodies would be invaluable.

Architects' leisure time, as I have said, is spent always being architects. They are fond of travel, and travel, especially abroad, means for them looking at buildings—and photographing them. Architects amass quantities of colour slides, which they do not often look at again except to project them in the evenings to gatherings of their friends, but since many of their friends are architects who have taken colour slides on their own holidays, the opportunities of showing them tend to be less frequent than the obligation to look at other people's. Colour slides are useful when talking to students or giving the kind of travel lecture architects are rather good at, and so taking them would be a harmless enough pursuit if there was not a suspicion that the very fact of photographing a building, and fussing over viewpoints and exposures, prevents the photographer from actually looking at it, or at least from examining it intensely enough with his own eyes to take in all it has to offer.

Even when the architect's off-duty pursuits are unconnected with buildings, they are still chosen for the sake of their appeal to instincts that are peculiarly his. Architects are fond of skiing and sailing—both of which involve discipline and the mastery of technique—and especially sailing, in which many of the attributes an architect is trained to respect are brought into play: the mastery, again, of certain skills, the control of inanimate forces and the precise planning and calculation required when navigating. A sailing boat, besides being beautiful, resembles a work of architecture; its compact design, without superfluous material, in which everything is there to do a job is, for him, architecture idealised. Related to these instincts is no doubt the architect's liking for well tuned motor cars, and especially vintage cars, which a remarkable number of architects own. An architect is usually a good driver.

Partly because of the expense of their education and the time it takes—the architect who perseveres with the orthodox course of school training is twenty-four or twenty-five before he can start to earn his living—architects, like other professional men and women, tend to come from the middle class, though not invariably so in these days of widely available student grants. This has the disadvantage of giving many architects little experience of how the majority of people live, and too many architects appear from their designs to assume that other people's tastes are the same as their own.

Statistics suggest that architecture is at the moment an ageing profession, but they may be misleading. In 1964 the average age of all the architects registered in Britain was 41. According to a RIBA survey made in 1970 it was by then 44, compared with 35 for university teachers, 37 for scientists and 39 for engineers, but the difference can partly be explained by the longer training architecture requires; an architect is probably at least 24 by the time he is qualified, and the other professions are likely to contain a higher proportion of younger men and women.

Architecture is also, just now, a fast growing profession. It was forecast in 1969 that the number of architects in Britain would increase by 22 per cent—nearly a quarter—during the subsequent ten years, and this has in fact happened so far; but an increase at anything like this rate will not continue. After the exceptionally large number who registered as architects in the early 1950s—that is, when things returned to normal after the war—reach retiring age in the mid-1980s the growth in numbers will slow down. In any case the supply of architects is far from outrunning the demand.

Apart from those described above, the personal characteristics of the architect are no different from those of most professional men. Architects are, on the whole, a well intentioned group. They more often hold left-wing views than workers in other professions because they have been trained to believe in planning and therefore instinctively oppose the laisser-faire philosophy of the right-wing capitalist and politician. Among their personal peculiarities are, again as a result of their training, a preference for conveying ideas graphically: when asked to explain something an architect will take out a pencil and do so with the aid of a diagram instead of verbally. This characteristic goes back at least as far as Sir Christopher Wren. In his biography of Wren, Sir John Summerson writes that he 'seems to have rather disliked writing—as a cumbrous necessity. His own writings are rarely elegant. He preferred to explain himself in models and diagrams and herein, perhaps, was an important factor in his eventual desertion of science for architecture'.

The modern architect, perhaps for this reason, is not usually very good at expressing himself in clear English, written or spoken, and as a result discussion meetings among architects are often rambling and confused.

Because of the understandings they share with them, architects feel an affinity with painters and sculptors, whom they frequently number among their friends. They buy the work of artists when they can afford to, and persuade their clients to buy it to embellish buildings they design. Drawing of a kind is one of their constant preoccupations, whether to explain ideas or to record facts and impressions; and yet, in spite of often being adept at making

71

sketches and handling the artist's materials, architects seldom achieve real quality if they attempt creative, as distinct from illustrative, art. They are perhaps inhibited by the fact that for them drawing is habitually used as a means to quite a different kind of end.

Architects are on the whole ambitious, though not necessarily with the expectation of making a lot of money. They are ambitious only in the sense of seeking the satisfactions of progress and achievement. You do not often find architects content simply to do the minimum that will bring them a living. The architect's daily routine is discussed later; but the life of which this routine is, as it were, the practical portion varies greatly according to the kind of practice he conducts (if he is a private architect) and where he conducts it. If he has a salaried post in an office, his work is much the same whether the office is a private or a public authority one, but the architect who runs his own office may have a small practice in a country town or be a partner in a large city practice or something in between.

He may or he may not specialise. If he works in a relatively small way, and outside one of the big cities, he can seldom afford to do so. He will want to take on any work that comes along, especially at first, when getting known and building up local connections are what his future depends on. He will find himself with small jobs—minor conversions and the like—that are neither very interesting nor very profitable, but he will tell himself that it is good policy to take them on because they may lead to something more important; that if he has taken trouble when asked to design a small addition to a workshop he may be remembered if its proprietor decides in due course to build a whole new factory.

In fact if an architect in, for example, a small town or a country district earns the reputation of being the man to go to when building is needed in that locality he will be sure of a regular flow of work. He will be like the local doctor, called in as a matter of course when a doctor's services are needed. And this will be good not only for the architect but for architecture, for there is an urgent need for more architects—especially architects with really high standards—focusing their efforts on particular localities for the well-being of which they assume a degree of responsibility. Architects have become too far removed from the day-to-day needs of individual towns and cities, and tend therefore to impose their designs on them instead of designing with knowledge and understanding of how they are growing and developing.

The current concern about the quality of the environment makes architects' involvement with places especially important and the comparison with doctors closely relevant; that is, with the family doctor who, over a long period, gets to know the people he looks after, their family life, their medical histories, their problems. He looks after local patients and no others. The architect could similarly develop a long-term relationship with one area, becoming familiar with every street, every tree, every lamp-post and boundary wall. He should know his area's history, how it has developed, what the needs of its occupants are, what changes are taking place in it and in what direction it is moving. Again like the family doctor he should be on the watch for new symptoms and, by associating himself closely with the local planners, for the evolution of new needs that may exercise an influence on his area—new road proposals, for example—so as to be ready with ideas and solutions to problems yet to arise.

This would mean working where he lives, like the doctor does, and not normally concerning himself with building anywhere else —an unattainable and not wholly practical notion perhaps, but one that, if kept in mind as an ideal, would put the role of the architect in relation to the environment into a better perspective. He, along with the planner, has more influence on the changing environment than anyone else, and so it is desirable that new buildings in any given area should be designed by an architect intimately involved with it; yet as things are at present it is a matter of chance where the architect of a new building comes from; he may never have visited the area before being given the job and may never go there again after completing it.

If the principle I am recommending here were followed, the architect would have to forget about the prestige of having a nationwide practice, but no doctor thinks he loses prestige by having all his patients close to where he lives. And those who employ architects would have to think differently too; a client now chooses an architect for reasons quite unconnected with his knowledge of the locality where building is to take place. He would have to be educated to look for an architect established in, and personally concerned with the future of, that locality, and also to feel that local knowledge matters.

But I am, alas, looking a long time ahead. Meanwhile at least we have the local *authority* architects, responsible for the public service buildings like schools and council houses, who are working in an area they know and are—or should be—in constant touch with the town planners responsible for the same area. The best of these do create some feeling of the local building programme being determined by local needs, but their range of building types is limited and their area of operations—the county or the county borough, or at the very smallest the urban or rural district council*—is too large to ensure their work being based on truly local knowledge. The need is not simply for Manchester architects to build in Manchester and Sussex architects in Sussex; that would bring no environmental improvement unless they were deeply rooted in one limited locality—in quite a small group of streets or cluster of villages—and felt a sense of long-term responsibility for co-ordinating and anticipating its needs.

This is the ideal for everyday building needs, but of course there are in addition building needs of a special, occasional and perhaps more monumental kind: civic centres, hospitals, churches, theatres, railway and air terminals, that provide as it were the architectural punctuation marks—the islands that stand out from the sea of routine and necessary construction—on which many architects' ambitions are focused because they offer more scope for original thought and opportunity for self-expression. There

* But see the footnotes on pages 22 and 32.

74

is excuse for these standing out from the rest and for their being designed by architects brought in from outside (though even they might do well to consult locally established architects, in addition to the local planners, about matters of siting and the appropriate use of materials); and there is the more reason for making public buildings a special case: they often require specialised designing experience.

CHAPTER FIVE

Opportunities and Rewards

The special experience required for designing some categories of building brings me back to the subject of the various types of practice the architect, and the assistants—mostly themselves qualified architects—who work in his office, may engage in. I have written of the small-town or country practice with its varied range of work—in the ideal situation local work; and of course there are small mixed practices in the big cities too, most often run by young architects who are still making their way. But the larger city practices often specialise: concentrate, that is, wholly or largely on one type of building.

They may do this from choice, because the architect or group of architects in charge of the practice is personally interested in, say, hospitals or factories; more likely they have become specialists through acquiring a reputation for some particular type of building so that one commission leads to another, a situation that may of course have come about as a result of their taking up a particular line in the first place. It is natural that an individual client, or a board of directors or governors, when seeking an architect to design a hospital or bank or theatre, should go to someone who has done a similar building before and knows the problems, and it is probably true that the more buildings of the same type any one architect designs, the better he becomes at it—but not necessarily so; he may get into a rut and assume that his way of solving a familiar problem is the only way, and someone coming to it with a fresh mind may open up new lines of development.

In any case to restrict the choice of architect to one who already has experience of the type of building required is in the long run a self-defeating principle because no young architect would ever gain the necessary experience. A better policy is for clients to judge by, and architects to try to demonstrate, all round ability rather than know-how in a particular field. The most successful architects are those who obtain successive commission from the same satisfied client, or whose name is recommended by a satisfied client to a new one. A satisfied client, architects do well to remember, is not only one who likes the building he gets but one who finds that it costs no more than the architect said it would and is completed by the promised date.

Time and cost are particularly important with commercial buildings like offices, factories and shops; rents will be lost or production or business held up if there are delays either in the legal and other preliminaries or in the actual construction, and the architects specialising in buildings of this type are often valued by their clients only because of their ability to conduct operations efficiently and speedily. I have already explained that the low standard of design all too evident in the majority of commercial buildings, especially blocks of offices, is due to property developers and speculators giving their patronage to a relatively small number of architectural firms solely because of their experience of site-development and of the business side of building operations. Some of the most prosperous architects specialise to the extent of doing nothing but big-city buildings for property developers.

Architects may specialise for many reasons, some of them rather unexpected; for example a couple of generations ago, when public buildings were frequently the subject of architectural competitions, there were several architects who specialised in town halls simply because they had acquired to a high degree the skills required for winning first place in a competition (a mixture

77

of genuine designing ability, an instinct for knowing what a particular assessor would go for, a facility for illustrating designs appealingly and an acute sense of what was fashionable without being noticeably so). The result was that a new town hall came their way every year or two.

Specialisation, however, even though it is often motivated by opportunity, is usually a matter of preference. An architect with a flair for interior design, colour and furnishing, may gradually find himself specialising in interiors. Another with a flair for operating on the broadest scale—for laying out buildings on the ground, for manipulating outdoor spaces and levels and using vegetation imaginatively—may become an architect-planner, developing new towns or housing estates and acting as the link between the town planner proper, who will probably hold some official post, and the numerous architects of the separate buildings on the site. He will then probably need to have a town-planning, as well as an architectural, degree.

Alternatively an architect may be interested in old buildings and their history and the materials and techniques used in them, and find himself specialising in restoration and conservation. With the present interest in conserving the areas of towns in which the traditional character remains, and with the greater care and respect accorded nowadays to historic buildings of all kinds, the need for architects with the highly specialised knowledge required to restore and maintain them has become greater; also the ability to adapt them to new uses, which is often the only practicable way of retaining a valuable old building no longer needed for its original purpose. This can be done successfully only by someone who knows and understands how it was first put together and who possesses the necessary aesthetic judgement—judgement dependent on scholarship as well as taste.

A senior architect who already has a reputation as a sensible and level-headed man sometimes finds himself specialising in a somewhat different sense: being asked to act as consultant when for some reason the application of another trained mind would be useful to the design of a building. This is sometimes required when a competition has been won by a young and inexperienced architect, when for some other reason the appointed architect is thought to need more experienced guidance or when several adjoining projects that are in the hands of different architects need co-ordinating.

Firms and institutions, or corporations such as the new towns, also sometimes appoint consultant architects to whom they can turn for guidance. In the case of new towns this can be nearly a full-time job, involving long-term planning and control of architectural standards generally, and can thus be rewarding; but a consultant otherwise is in an unsatisfactory position in having only partial and delayed control of an undertaking in which the initial decisions count for much. The Royal Fine Art Commission sometimes recommends the appointment of a consultant when it examines a design that it thinks not up to standard but feels unable to suggest replacing the architect by a better one. This course seldom brings good results; one architect trying to modify the work of another at best produces a compromise. He certainly cannot turn a dull designer into an imaginative one.

For all kinds of specialisation the full architectural training is essential, since the basic principles of design and construction are the same however they are applied. The specialist architect must be totally equipped, just as the doctor specialising in gynaecology must start by being a complete doctor and know how to set a broken leg. Specialisation, as I have pointed out, has both its virtues and its drawbacks, and it is by no means necessary in practice for even the most businesslike firm of architects to specialise. Many do not, and occupy themselves with all kinds of work in whatever variety it comes along. There is only one type of building a large office or a senior architect is seldom willing to take on: that is a private house.

The reason is solely that the amount of work involved in designing a house is greater than in any other type of building in relation to its cost, both because of the time taken to plan it to fit in with the idiosyncratic wishes of the client and, more especially, because of the number of detailed drawings that have to be prepared. In many other types of building the architect can—with advantage to him and to the efficiency of the building—use many of the same details that he has used before and found satisfactory: ways of finishing off parapets and handrails, door-frames and window-heads. These can often be standardised throughout the building and the drawings required are therefore easily produced. With a private house every room is different and the details for every room have to be specially designed and drawn out. This makes a lot of work, but since a house is a relatively inexpensive building and since an architect's fees are calculated as a percentage of the cost, his fees for designing a house are too small to make it worth while. There is probably more work for the architect in a house costing £10,000 (for which his fees will be between £600 and £1,000—see my explanation below of the obligatory fee scales) than in, say, a school costing £50,000 for which his fees will be around £3,000.

An architect with a big practice has to keep a constant watch not only on the relationship in general between running costs and fees but on the running cost of every job to make sure he is not spending more on it than the fees it will earn allow. Each draughtsman or assistant fills in a time-sheet to show how many hours have been spent on each job, and the office overheads—rent, lighting and heating, postage and telephone bills, the cost of drawing materials and of printing drawings—as well as salaries, are apportioned accordingly. By this means he knows how well a job is paying, and he will almost certainly find that a house is not paying at all.

This does not mean that no eminent or successful architect ever designs a house. He may do so to please a friend even if he has to do it at a loss, or to oblige a client from whom he gets other, more profitable, work or hopes to get work. He may design one because he enjoys doing so; perhaps there is some idea he wants to try out—a house is a personal affair and close collaboration with a client who is interested and enterprising makes it an ideal occasion for experiment. The architect may sometimes take on a house to fill an interval between larger jobs. It is better to keep assistants at work, even uneconomically, than to keep them idle or have to fire them—and then probably find them not available when the office is busy again.

Nevertheless in a big office of the kind responsible for most large city buildings designing private houses would be unthinkable. Houses are done by some architects with mixed practices working outside the big cities, but chiefly by the younger architects. They can no more afford to take on a job that does not pay than a senior architect, but the difference is that their overheads are less.

The high rent and rates in a big city, the cost of paying at least a minimum staff even when they are not fully stretched and all the expenses of running a large office, add up to something of quite a different order from the expenses of a small—especially an out-of-town—practice. And what counts for more, a young architect or one who keeps his office to a moderate size probably does most of the designing himself, whereas an architect in a big way spends much of his time as an administrator. An architect with a small office may even do much of the drawing himself, and so avoid having to pay out large sums in draughtsmen's salaries.

A lot of very good work is done by small offices consisting of one or two architects, perhaps a couple of assistants or draughtsmen and a secretary. They may not have the resources to handle large commercial and industrial projects—and may not want to—but clients often prefer dealing with architects of this modest kind because they are sure of the personal attention of the architect himself; dealing with a big office they may meet him at the beginning and thereafter only see a junior partner or associate.

Some types of building can without harm be dealt with impersonally; some need the touch of the individual; but in all cases the quality of the architecture depends eventually on the architect in charge. However far we may go in getting calculations done, and even alternative plan arrangements appraised, by computers, personal judgements come into it sooner or later and are in fact what architecture, as distinct from mere construction, is about. During the process of designing even the most highly 'functional' building there are many decisions to be taken, and these can be taken intelligently or carelessly, sensitively or insensitively. How they are taken will make or mar the building both as an object to be admired or not and as one that serves its occupants well or badly.

This makes the personality, sensitivity and experience of the architect vital. He is not only a cog in the immensely complicated machine required to get a modern building off the ground, but is a unique individual, with qualities different from other individuals, and it is therefore important for a client—whether this means a prospective building owner or some kind of board or committee —to know the architect and exactly what his personal attributes are. For this reason one custom accepted nowadays in the profession is obviously undesirable: the custom whereby firms of architects operate under the names of men long since dead, whose work may bear no relation to that which made those names famous in the first place. The practice may have been sold to a newcomer or carried on by a son (without any check on whether he has inherited his father's talent) or even by a head draughtsman after the architect's death.

A client going to such a firm probably does so because of its reputation, but if the individuals who earned it that reputation have been replaced by others who may be incapable of designing buildings of the same quality—buildings the client has looked at before choosing an architect—is he not likely to be defrauded? It is no justification to say that lawyers have a tradition of handing down the names of firms from generation to generation; a lawyer's business is not, like an architect's, dependent on personal sensibilities. A better comparison would be with painters and sculptors, who would never consider allowing their sons-in-law, their ex-assistants or those who have taken on the lease of their studio to sign pictures or sculptures with their name. In the interest of the artistic integrity of the profession the Royal Institute of British Architects should institute a bylaw insisting that all firms of architects should bear the names of the people in charge of them—or at least not bear the names of people no longer in charge.

The above was by way of being an aside—but a necessary one—arising out of the question of a client's relationship with his architect, itself a product of the architect's position as a professional man. The RIBA is deeply involved in their relationship, partly because it formulates the rules by which it is conducted, but also because the qualifications and standards that membership of the RIBA signifies are the client's best guarantee that he will get a conscientious professional service from any member he employs. I have already referred to the need to improve standards, which in a theoretical way the RIBA is clearly aware of. Awareness of it throughout the profession was one cause of the heated controversy which followed the RIBA's proposal, a few years back, to change the system of professional suffixes.

For many years, as soon as a student had qualified as an architect he was entitled to place after his name the letters ARIBA (Associate of the Royal Institute of British Architects), and after being in practice for some years he was able to apply for promotion to FRIBA (F standing for Fellow, and indicating to potential clients and the public an architect of seniority and experience). There was also—though there are only a few of them left now—a third class of member, the LRIBA (L standing for Licentiate), indicating a member who has not passed the usual examinations but who has been admitted to membership after practising as an architect for at least ten years. The object of this class of membership was to avoid the unfairness of depriving of their living architects who were already in practice when examinations became obligatory, but no new applications for licentiateship have been accepted since 1955 and the Licentiate class is therefore dying out; any confusion caused by a class with dubious qualifications will soon be ended.

The difference between Associate and Fellow also caused a little confusion (the very word associate suggested someone who did not fully belong to the profession) and the feeling grew among RIBA members a few years ago that a single type of membership —signifying simply a qualified architect—would be more sensible. Proposals to bring this about were objected to by some Fellows who did not want to lose a privileged status and by many Associates who valued this designation because it showed proof that they had passed the necessary examinations (all Fellows had not done so; some had been promoted from being Licentiates). It was proposed that all should use the suffix MRIBA (M for Member), but on the objection being raised that this might be taken by a confused public as indicating still another class of architect, instead of embracing both classes, it was eventually decided to use simply the suffix RIBA in spite of the illogicality of describing a person as an institute. It was also ruled, however, that those who wished could continue to use A and F; so the confusion has not yet been resolved.

In earlier chapters I have discussed the kind of people architects are and how they are organised, but I have said nothing about the kind of living they earn: how rich a successful architect can expect to become and what sort of salary an architect in various grades of employment can count on. Architecture, like the rest of the professions, is not a thing to take up if the main objective in choosing a career is to make a lot of money quickly. It cannot in this sense compare with the Stock Exchange or with various forms of business and industry, and most architects embark on their career primarily because it is what they are interested in. Nevertheless it has at least one advantage even from the financial point of view: that, at the present time and throughout the foreseeable future, there is no surplus of architects.

Although Britain has a larger number of architects per head of population than most other countries (see Appendix 1), the demand for architects' services seems to keep them reasonably well employed in spite of occasional lean periods due to restrictions on capital expenditure, and in view of the fact that the country's present efforts to improve standards of housing, education, health and working conditions all involve new building programmes, this situation is likely to continue. No qualified architect, that is to say, so long as he is not particular about the quality of the buildings he is helping to create or about the level, in a private or public hierarchy, at which he works, need be unemployed for long.

He will not, however, make a fortune, unless he is both clever and lucky. There are a few successful architects with large practices who do become wealthy men—if not on the same scale as industrial magnates or property tycoons—but the rewards of architecture vary widely and the average architect does not expect riches; in fact a survey of the earnings of various professions and callings made by the RIBA in 1971 disclosed that architects were, along with university teachers, right at the bottom of the list. This disappointing situation is not so apparent at the beginning but emerges as the years go by. In the youngest age group (between twenty-five and twenty-nine—that is, soon after qualifying) the average architect's earnings were £2,125 a year, which compares with £2,375 earned by the average actuary and £3,000 by the barrister working in industry or for a commercial company, but with only £1,600 by the average university teacher, £1,647 by a works manager and £1,650 by a chartered insurance man; so that relatively the architect was not doing badly, perhaps because the shortage of young assistants created a demand which kept salaries at a reasonable level.

But in the higher age groups the architect was shown by the survey to fall back. The average architect between forty-five and forty-nine (the age when earnings, judged by this survey, seem to be highest) earned £3,236 while the actuary earned £5,250, the barrister in commerce or industry £5,140, the university teacher £3,550, the works manager £2,638 and the insurance man £2,610. After that age the average architect's earnings slowly declined but all the others continued to increase.

The average earnings irrespective of age, in another investigation covering the years 1966-70, were found to be £4,250 for actuaries and £4,514 for solicitors (counting principals only), but only £2,530 for university teachers and £2,553 for architects. Engineers, it should be added, have even lower average earnings except very late in their careers.

Architects, moreover, have less assurance of a steady income than most professional men. Because of the fluctuations in the amount of work available, due both to a continual rise and fall of expenditure on building—the national economy always seems to be the victim of stop-go policies—and to the disorganised way in which, as I have already described, work is allocated to particular architects, private architects are in a permanent state of uncertainty about how busy they are going to be next year—or even next month—and the public architectural offices, too, suffer from being unable to foresee a programme of work, and therefore to plan an appropriate staff intake, because of the way changes of government policy cause unpredictable demands and postponements. This means that public offices are often over-staffed, which is bad for morale as well as for the economical use of manpower. For private architects it means that prosperous periods have to see an office through lean periods.

Yet in spite of the foregoing comparisons with other professions, architects do on the whole earn a reasonable living as well as having an interesting life; its very unpredictability is at least a safeguard against dullness. And because there is always a demand for his services, the salaried assistant can move if he gets bored from one office to another, or even from a public office to a private one and back again, though he will do better to stick to the same office if he hopes for an eventual partnership in a private firm or a senior post with a public authority.

Assistants in both private and public offices are, of course, paid by salary, the former on average being somewhat better paid (at least in a small office, where they are likely to be given greater responsibility earlier in their career), but the latter having more security. The average salary of a newly qualified assistant was in 1973 around £2,300 a year, or perhaps a bit less if the office was outside London or one of the big cities.

An architect who stays on in the public service, whether in a local authority office* or in one of the central government departments like the Property Services Agency (the new name for the architects' department of the Ministry of Public Building and Works), or who works in a public corporation like the Post Office or the railways, has a reasonably well paid job (see the table in Appendix 3). From this table it can be observed that salaries in central government are higher than in local government. This is due partly to higher rates being paid in London, but also to the fact that architects in central government are older than those employed elsewhere and tend to be more specialised and highly qualified.

If the official architect rises right to the top he can hope eventually to earn between £7,000 and £8,000 a year. This is the present salary of the chief architect of one of the larger county councils or a big city council. There are a few official architectural posts, such as architect to the Greater London Council, that pay even more.

Not many private architects earn as much as this, though there are some, especially those concentrating on commercial and property development work, who must earn quite a lot more. Most, as the figures given above and in the appendix show, earn less, and no assistant in a private office earns anything like as much. Nowadays, however, the profits of private architectural practices, instead of going largely to the man at the top, are far more evenly

---

* Once again the reservation must be made (see footnotes in earlier chapters) that appointments of this kind will be affected by the reorganisation of local government due in 1974, though it is to be hoped that this will not result in a reduced status, and therefore a reduced level of remuneration, for local authority architects.

spread than they used to be because of the recent elaboration of the system, already referred to, of partnerships, associateships and the like.

The money earned by a private architectural office, which must pay the assistants' salaries and all the overheads and running expenses before it can be shared out among the partners and associates, comes wholly from fees. An architect is debarred by the RIBA's Code of Professional Practice from 'any other source of remuneration in connection with the works and duties entrusted to him' except his professional fee or, in the case of an employee (private or public), his salary. His fees are a percentage of the cost of the work, normally 6 per cent.

This 6 per cent is a minimum; that is, architects are not allowed to charge at a lower rate—undercutting each other's fees is one of the most serious professional crimes—but there is nothing in the Code of Professional Practice to stop them charging more, if they can find a client willing to pay more; in fact for small jobs (which involve more work in relation to the fee earned) they nearly always do pay more. The RIBA recommends charging the standard fee of 6 per cent of the cost only for buildings costing more than £16,000, and a gradual increase up to 10 per cent for buildings costing £2,000 or less.

There are two circumstances, however, in which architects are allowed to charge less than 6 per cent. One is if they provide less than the full professional service. For example if they design a building but the client then decides not to go ahead with it. The RIBA's official scale of fees lays down the percentage to be charged according to the work done—2 per cent if the architect has made the design and prepared an estimate of cost; 4.5 per cent if he has also done all the necessary drawings, and so on. The other special circumstance arises in connection with certain types of building involving a large degree of repetition, such as large housing schemes where a few types of houses are repeated a great many times, and some industrial buildings. If some reduction were not allowed, the fee for a factory covering large areas

88

of ground by multiplying the same simple structural element would, when charged at the full 6 per cent, be far too high in relation to the work required. Reduced fees for repetitive work are again strictly controlled by the RIBA.

The fees described above are of course all for new buildings, and the RIBA also lays down a special scale of fees for the alteration and conversion of existing buildings. In addition to the statutory fee, the architect may ask the client to pay travelling expenses (which may amount to a lot in the case of a large project in a different part of the country), and the client must pay separately the fees of consultants like engineers and quantity surveyors. To avoid sending a client demands for so many fees, there have been discussions about the desirability of one consolidated fee, which the architect would apportion by agreement among his professional colleagues.

It may be thought that the system of paying architects a percentage of the cost of the building might encourage them to be extravagant—the more expensive the building the larger the fee. But it does not in fact work out like that. An architect's prosperity and that of his office, depend, as I have already explained, on a continuous flow of work, which itself very largely depends on the reputation he earns for efficiency and for spending his client's money economically, and he will lose much more by being extravagant than he will gain by a bigger fee on just one job.

In addition, the amount of work he puts into a given job rests largely with him, and if he wanted to increase his earnings unscrupulously it would be easier for him to do the work in a slapdash way than to increase its cost—and his own work at the same time. The most uneconomical thing of all, from the architect's point of view, as well as the most irritating from the client's, is to allow the cost to creep up by making changes once the job has started. A great deal of extra work is required of him if variations have to be made from the original drawings and specifications.

In spite of all this, the present regulations that control an architect's charges were radically criticised, somewhat unexpectedly, by the Monopolies Commission when it investigated the architectural profession in 1969-70. The commission proposed in its report that the scale of fees laid down by the RIBA should no longer be mandatory; that is, that architects should be allowed to depart from it if they wished. This showed a surprising ignorance of how architects work on the part of such an experienced body of men, who were more accustomed no doubt to dealing with commerce and industry. Architects do not provide goods but services, and the thoroughness, skill and conscientiousness with which they perform these services rests with them. To allow some architects to provide these services more cheaply than others—in fact to legitimise fee-cutting—would mean that the most work went to the architect who was willing to skimp the quality of the work he did, either by not studying the problem thoroughly, giving less time to considering alternative ways of solving it, providing inadequate drawings or undertaking less supervision during construction. Only by failing his client in one of these ways could he afford to obtain work by offering to do it more cheaply than some of his colleagues, and this kind of competitiveness over fees would therefore lead to poorer quality architecture. The Monopolies Commission's report on architects seems to have been shelved for the present. If it is acted on, a sensible government is likely to ignore this particular recommendation.

Some architects find the discussion of fees with a prospective client embarrassing, especially in connection with a highly personal job like a private house, where the client-architect relationship should be that of personal friendship. This makes a pamphlet issued by the RIBA especially useful. It is called *Conditions of Engagement and Scale of Professional Charges* and explains both an architect's duties and a client's rights. If the client is given a copy at the outset of a job, all the questions about how he pays his architect and what for, when the payments are due and what expenses in addition to his fees an architect can claim, are answered without the risk of misunderstandings.

Other countries than Britain, it should be mentioned, have different systems, the most remarkable—a system that avoids all dealings about fees between architect and client—being the Spanish. The client deals only with the College of Architects—in many ways the equivalent of the RIBA—which charges him whatever fees are due, and the architect is paid his fee by the college.

So much for the financial rewards of architecture. But perhaps the first question a young architect will ask before embarking on his career is not shall I make a fortune, but shall I become famous? The answer to this is: not very, however successful you are, because architecture is not an activity in which the public (or the newspapers and television programmes that help form public opinion) takes much interest, in spite of the degree to which it affects everyone's daily life. This may be the fault of architecture having become too much a professional mystery, it may be the result of the literary, as distinct from the visual, bias in most people's education and of school education not including the appreciation of architecture, or it may be due to other factors—some of which I have discussed elsewhere in this book.

Architects continually—and justly—complain that when a photograph of a new building appears in the newspapers, the caption almost never gives the name of the architect, whereas it would be unthinkable for a painting or work of sculpture to be reproduced with no mention of the name of the artist. This is indeed unfair, but it only underlines the fact that architects are not news. A paper's news editor feels it his duty to provide the information his readers want. If they see a reproduction of an interesting-looking painting they say 'I wonder who did that' and would complain if they were not told; but no ordinary news-paper reader, on seeing a photograph of a building, says 'I wonder who designed that'. Architects will not get the recognition they would like until they can make what they do seem interesting and something in which the public is positively involved.

Meanwhile it remains a fact, regrettable though it may be, that architects do not become well known public figures—or very seldom. Ask a man in the street for the name of a leading architect and he is unlikely to be able to recall one, though he could probably recall the name of a leading scientist or novelist or musician. There are of course well known architects—even architects who become, through their inventiveness or ability to attract the limelight, cult figures. But they are cult figures and known personalities only among other architects. It would be better all round if architects were less turned in on themselves.

CHAPTER SIX

Learning Architecture

Most architects now in practice will have spent a good part, if not all, of their training period in an architectural school. But this was not so in the past; in fact school training is comparatively recent. The first British architectural school of any kind was set up at the Architectural Association in London in 1847, and the first full-time school, also at the AA, in 1901 (the 1847 enterprise only provided evening classes for young architects working in offices in the daytime). A second full-time school was started as part of Liverpool University a year or two later, and a third as part of London University soon afterwards. Others followed quickly, either in universities or in municipal colleges of art or polytechnics. Now there are thirty-one schools in Britain (see Appendix 4) which provide a full qualifying course usually occupying five years. The AA school, by far the largest in Britain with about 400 students at any one time, is the only one that has, with difficulty, remained independent. The thirty-one schools produce between them about 800 new architects every year.

Before the foundation of all these schools, the normal way of training to be an architect was by becoming a pupil in an office. It was not in fact until the 1920s that school training almost wholly supplanted the pupilage system. The latter at its best had certain advantages, notably the personal nature of the tuition.

The aspirant architect enrolled in an office as an articled pupil. He (in practice normally his parents) paid the architect a fee, and the pupil undertook to remain for a certain length of time, after which the architect would certify that he had reached the required level of competence and then he could embark on the next stage of his career.

Eminent architects were able to ask large sums for accepting young men as pupils, and there was competition to become a pupil in the most fashionable offices, which gave the young architect a status that was useful for years afterwards. A particular tradition of design, or expertise in various styles, was passed on in this way from master to pupil, which encouraged continuity but also perhaps fostered conservatism. Whether the pupilage system was also a good method of education depended of course on whether the architect was a good teacher and how conscientiously he fulfilled his side of the bargain.

There were some who took advantage of it, treating the pupil simply as cheap labour and leaving him to pick up information as best he could. There were others who took their responsibility seriously, and then the young architect had the advantage of being taught in a place where architecture was actually being done and thus learning the practical side—the running of an office and the successive stages of creating a building—at the same time as the theoretical.

This advantage was lost when the full-time schools first took over: their courses were wholly academic and the students gained no practical experience and were given no contact with actual building operations. Nor were they even asked to design buildings until the later stages of the course, with the result that some students might discover, after several years spent studying architecture, that they lacked the design instinct, the discriminating eye and the ability to visualise things in three dimensions which, though far from being the whole of architecture, are qualities the good architect must possess.

When I myself entered a school of architecture in the 1920s,

94

the first two years of the course were occupied with learning the classical orders and drawing elaborate compositions incorporating the orders and other elements of various past styles, with learning architectural lettering (especially the Roman incised lettering used on Trajan's column), with learning how shadows were cast on to geometrical forms (in fact not at all a bad way of getting accustomed to seeing objects in three dimensions), with learning the rules of perspective and elementary mathematics and with drawing out the structural parts from which simple conventional buildings are made—for example the various kinds of bond in which bricks can be laid and the arrangement of timbers used to construct a dormer window. Only during the third year were we allowed to try our hands at some elementary problem in design, such as adding a porch to an existing house, and only at the end of that year did we begin designing buildings.

This may have been a good grounding of a traditional kind, but it was wholly unrealistic. Even when, in the later years, we were made to design more ambitious buildings they were far removed from the sort of buildings a young architect—indeed any architect—would be likely to meet with in real life. I recall spending weeks designing an embassy on a rocky promontory. The designs, moreover, were judged nearly as much by the way they were presented as by their architectural merits; a lot of our time was spent laying graduated water-colour washes to furnish our drawings with dramatic skies, or decorating the plans with elaborate floor patterns to underline the relative significance of the different spaces—in the style established many years before at the Beaux Arts school in Paris.

It is easy, however, to caricature this highly academic method of architectural education. Considered in the light of the historical attitude to architecture itself prevalent at the time—an attitude that was to undergo a revolutionary change within a dozen years —it did provide a sense of the perspective of architecture going back into history and an appreciation of the humanistic value of architecture as one of the liberal arts, which a student plunged straight into the day-to-day realities of architectural practice would never have obtained. And there are arguments in favour of using the student years to think big and develop the imagination even in somewhat unrealistic directions, since the opportunity to do this may not arise later. Nevertheless, the result of this remote and wholly theoretical curriculum was to produce young architects quite unfitted to make themselves useful as assistants in offices when they reached the next stage of their careers.

Busy architects complained that if they took on school-trained assistants, especially those trained in the longer established architectural schools such as the AA school in London and those attached to universities, they found them ignorant of the practical business that working in an office largely consists of, and incapable of quickly and efficiently producing the working drawings that it is the principal job of a junior assistant to prepare. The architect had to carry the school-trained assistant for months if not years, as little more than a passenger, while he learnt, by watching and helping others, the common-sense skills of day-to-day practice; and the architect was often—no doubt still is— irritated to find the junior assistant straight from architectural school wanting to be the designer rather than a draughtsman and apt to argue with him about the merits of his own designs. Yet, once again, if you cannot have arrogant and ambitious ideas when you are a student, when can you have them?

The students from the less pretentious schools—the polytechnics and the like—were more immediately useful because they had a more down-to-earth curriculum and catered more consciously (the class stratification of English society had its influence here as it did everywhere else) for the student aiming at a good post as an assistant than for the student who regarded such a post only as a necessary step towards becoming an independent architect. But even these students found they had much more to learn after entering an office, thereby demonstrating that however practical and realistic a school training may be, many of the qualities necessary to a good architect can be acquired only in the office and on the site, in fact by experience of actual building.

The realisation of this led to radical changes being made in the system of school education, and today architectural schools are very different. One difference of course is that, since the appearance of buildings is no longer based on the historic styles, these are not studied to the same extent; in fact in some schools the history of architecture is not studied at all, which is regrettable. Knowledge of the past is important to an architect not in order that he shall imitate it but in order that he shall understand the principles on which architecture has always been founded and see towns and cities as part of a continuous evolutionary process.

However, the far more important differences between architectural schools of the old type and the new—between those of the 1920s and, say, the 1950s onwards—lie in the efforts that have been made to devise programmes of study that bring the student into closer touch with the realities of building; also, in the last few years only, in the efforts to break down the barriers that separate the architect from other specialists with whom he will have to co-operate.

With regard to the first, one of the most important steps forward, apart from a general move towards a more practical curriculum and more sensible subjects for design programmes, was taken by the Birmingham School of Architecture in the 1950s when it instituted what were called 'live projects'. By this was meant the undertaking of actual commissions by groups of senior students under the supervision of the school staff. They went through the whole sequence of operations, from discussing the project with the client to supervising construction on the site, just as though they were already practising architects, and thus learnt about each stage by direct experience. There was naturally some resentment at this experiment on the part of local architects, who regarded it as unfair competition, but the school strictly obeyed the rules of the profession against undercutting fellow architects' fees, charging the client who had been bold or public-spirited enough to commission a building on this basis the full fees and using the money on behalf of the school.

Now most schools of architecture find some way of incorporating experience of real building in their curriculum, as well as repeated visits to building sites, which in my day as a student were almost unknown. And the whole structure of school education has been changed in order to alternate practical with theoretical study. Instead of five years spent continuously in the school, the normal procedure today is three years in the school, a break of one year spent working in an architect's office and then the two final years, from which the student can gain greater benefit with a year's practical experience behind him.

And even after these two years, and after passing the final examination at the end of them, he is still not a qualified architect. He must have two more years of office experience and then pass a separate examination in 'professional practice' (by which is meant such subjects as office administration, building codes and contracts and all the legal and financial matters architects have to know about). Only after this can he be admitted as an ARIBA. In the 1920s there was no such examination; only the need to spend six months in an office after the five years spent in an architectural school.

As regards preparing the student for the less isolated and individualistic way of working characteristic of the modern architect, the schools have introduced a number of modifications to the old Beaux Arts-type system. One is the system of group working, by which teams of students tackle a problem collectively—both the research needed before embarking on the design of a building and the design itself. They share the various tasks among themselves, just like the teams in charge of individual jobs in the better organised public offices. Another modification is the inclusion, right at the beginning of the course, at least in some schools, of a preliminary course dealing with the basic principles of design, of the use of materials, of elementary structures and so on, suitable for other students besides students of architecture.

If students of engineering, industrial design, town planning and architecture—and perhaps also of painting and sculpture—share such a course in common, they not only learn co-operation with each other but they acquire a common understanding of design principles: a visual language, as it were, that will make future co-operation easier.

Another advantage of such a preliminary course, which is at present most frequently found in colleges of art and design, is that students can use the time it occupies to decide which branch of design they are best fitted for; having started with the intention of becoming architects or industrial designers or engineers they can switch from one profession to another without having to abandon a specialised course on which they have already embarked and start again at the beginning.

What is called multi-disciplinary education is a direct result of the need in present-day circumstances, to which I referred in Chapter 1, for the various professions to work closely together, and a typical sign of the times was a recent decision by University College, London, to unite several of its departments—those of architecture, town planning and some branches of engineering and building science—into one super-department called the School of Environmental Studies, thus providing obvious opportunities for the exchange of staff and programmes.

More experiments of this kind are certainly on the way, and will be assisted by the closer association of schools of architecture with universities. At an important conference on architectural education that was held at Oxford in 1968 it was decided as a matter of future policy that schools of architecture should be within universities whenever possible. At present, of the thirty-one British schools, thirteen are departments of universities, the remainder, apart from the independent AA school, being in art colleges or polytechnics, which also offer an opportunity of organising multi-disciplinary courses, though in a more limited range of subjects.

Universities, in addition, are in a stronger position to arrange for post-graduate study. Some years ago most post-graduate architectural students were studying town planning because the only courses offering a planning qualification to architects were those that followed on after the full five-year architecture course; but although separate planning courses are now established at several universities, there is an increasing amount of post-graduate activity among architects, either pursuing specialist studies or doing research.

I have been writing so far as if school training was nowadays the only form of architectural education, but although the old system of articled pupilage has altogether disappeared it is still possible to qualify as an architect without attending an architectural school. Quite a number manage to do so—choosing this method for their own reasons but seldom nowadays for the reason that used to be commonest: that they, or their parents, could not afford the school fees which can sometimes be as much as £400 a year. In these days of local authority grants, most young people who want to study architecture can enter one of the schools provided they have reached the necessary educational standard— normally five GCE passes (including English and mathematics or a science subject), two of which must be at Advanced ('A') level. Two A-level passes are in any case required for university entry. There is some competition for the places available, but it is severe only in the schools with the highest reputation and the greatest prestige.

Qualifying outside an architectural school is, however, very hard work. The usual procedure is to get employment in an architect's office, at first of course in a very junior capacity, and to pick up there whatever useful information the work makes available, in any case learning draughtsmanship and the practical side of professional life. The rest must be studied in the student's spare time, from books, lectures and evening classes. When he is ready for it he can take the intermediate examination—equivalent to the examination taken in the schools at the end of the third year—and in due course the final examination—equivalent to that at the end of the fifth year. But it is not easy, doing a full-time job as well as studying for examinations, especially because he also has to prepare 'testimonies of study', which are special sets of drawings equivalent to the design projects undertaken in the schools, to present to the examiners at the same time as he sits the written examination.

These 'external' examinations are conducted by the RIBA who make sure their standard is on a level with that of the schools. The students in the schools do not take the same examination papers. The schools are very sensibly given the freedom of action to arrange their curricula and methods of teaching in whatever way they think best, each school however being periodically inspected by the RIBA's Board of Architectural Education to make sure its standards and results are good enough. If they are, the school is granted exemption from the RIBA's intermediate and final examinations. These are the only examinations recognised by the Architects' Registration Council and therefore giving admission to the architects' register. There are a few schools of architecture recognised by the RIBA for exemption up to inter-mediate level only, and a student attending one of these can either move on to do the final two years in another school or move on to an office and take his final examination externally.

The one advantage of learning to be an architect by working in an office and taking the external examinations must be clear from what I have said already about students leaving the schools with so much still to learn about the realities of day-to-day practice. To start with one's feet already firmly on the ground at least avoids the difficult adjustment that follows five years of thinking about architecture as the basis of the arts and as a means of reforming the world; it avoids the need to educate oneself at so late a stage as a decision-making individual.

The main disadvantage, apart from missing the carefully balanced curriculum of the schools and the experienced supervision of studies provided there, is having to do without the stimulating company of fellow students and the exchange of ideas with them.

Many people have found that, even in the best equipped schools, they learn more from their fellow students than from the staff appointed to instruct them.

Architecture can thus be learnt in different ways: wholly at one of the schools, wholly by experience in an office combined with private study, or by some combination of the two. It is desirable that plenty of alternatives should be available and it would be a pity if the development of school training were to oust all other methods. The old-fashioned style of pupilage is unlikely to return, but it might be worth experimenting with a new form of pupilage that has not yet been tried—not as a replacement of school training but as an alternative available to those whom it would suit better. By this I mean some form of pupilage within the big *public* offices. Public authorities are in many ways the modern patrons, fulfilling the role the wealthy individual fulfilled a century ago, and architectural offices like those of the Greater London Council, the Ministry of Public Building and Works and the major counties and county boroughs could well accept some responsibility for the training of young architects, perhaps in conjunction with the local education authority. Aspiring architects, after a short preliminary course elsewhere, could be enrolled as working pupils and given practical experience and specific tuition at the same time. It is an idea worth considering.

Finally, before leaving the subject of education I should re-emphasise that the education of an architect never stops—or should never stop. Perhaps one can identify the alarming number of second-quality architects the profession contains with those who think that once they have acquired the right letters after their name they have finished with having to learn. It is not only that, like doctors, architects have continually to keep themselves up to date (the AA School of Architecture in London has, among other places, instituted refresher courses for practising architects with this in mind); it is also that, by its very nature, architecture is an art and a profession in which no limit can be set to the benefits gained by continued study. The best architects go on learning all their lives.

There are two main ways in which architects learn more, after the specifically educational phases of their careers are over and they are qualified to practise: by observation and by experience. Observation means looking at buildings, and the architect with the inquiring mind that all good architects should have is always studying and analysing buildings, old and new (hence his fondness, already referred to, for foreign travel), and storing away in his mind the lessons he learns from them and the variety of example—functional, technical and aesthetic—that they provide.

But the key to learning is experience. An architect learns most by building, and a good architect never repeats his successes but is breaking new ground for himself with every new project—widening his repertoire and deepening his understanding. Theory will not get him far unless it is backed by practical experience, which explains why the architectural schools insist that most, if not all, of the teaching staff should also be practising architects. In other departments of universities and polytechnics it may be better that the teaching should be done by professional peda-gogues, for whom teaching is itself their trade; but architecture is not one of them. In some schools of architecture the head (or the professor, if the school is part of a university) may make this his full-time job, but even he will certainly have had experience as an architect before devoting himself to teaching. Most of his staff will teach only part-time and run architectural offices at the same time. Sometimes the head manages to do this too. Amateur-ish teaching techniques do not matter nearly as much as failure to bring students into touch with reality, and a school with too many full-time teachers soon finds itself cut off from the conditions in which architecture is always being put to the test—and then it begins to lose the confidence of its students.

Conversely, the more the teaching at a school can be integrated with the practice of architecture the healthier and more effective it will become. Apart from the 'live projects' already mentioned, the students can be involved in the research required for projects the staff are engaged on in their own offices, so that research is linked to real problems and its application can be studied. Lecturers can be brought in to talk about work they are engaged on, and visiting architects can be invited in to criticise the students' completed projects, regarding them not as academic exercises but in relation to the responsible work of an architect. Existing buildings, too, can be studied from the user's point of view and judged according to the satisfaction it gives him, which may be very different from the satisfaction it gives its designer.

CHAPTER SEVEN

The Daily Round

For the purpose of giving, in this chapter, a picture of how the architect and his staff spend their working day I shall take a typical medium-size private office with two partners in charge of it and a staff of about twenty. This is a good size for an office where the partners want to remain fully responsible for the designs produced and to do most of the basic designing themselves; that is, to diagnose the client's needs, make the initial sketches for him to approve and take responsibility for the general form and character of the design, leaving only the details to be worked out, and the constructional drawings to be prepared, by assistants under their supervision.

If they allow the office to grow larger—if they take on more work and therefore make it necessary to employ a larger staff of assistants—they will be less in touch personally with every job because they will have to spend more time on administration, and even if the work does not suffer (which it need not do if they have fully capable senior assistants), it will not have the individual character they would bring to it themselves—the character, perhaps, that made the client choose this particular firm in the first place.

An alternative is to create more partners as the size of the firm expands, either by promoting senior staff or by joining up with other architects in the same situation, and then working out a system (as already described) whereby the partners take basic decisions collectively and afterwards delegate the work on each project to a team of assistants, each responsible to a partner or associate. There are firms organised in this way, and achieving a high standard of design and quality of service, which employ as many as 80 or 100 assistants. There are some firms with an even larger number, but they are mostly the big commercial offices working for property developers and the like, and have more the character of plan-producing factories than places where the art of architecture is conscientiously pursued.

There are also, of course, many firms with only one architect in charge, but it is generally found convenient to operate with at least two partners, so that there is always someone in charge of the office if one partner has to be absent—visiting clients or sites, taking part in one of the many professional meetings or conferences through which architects exchange ideas and endlessly discuss professional politics, on holiday or ill. Besides this, many architects find it helpful to have someone at an equal level with whom they can discuss problems; the best ideas often emerge out of arguments and mutual criticism.

An office with twenty assistants will not be too unwieldy and yet will be big enough to encompass a fairly wide range of work. As well as new buildings it may have a few conversion or alteration jobs which a large commercial office would not be bothered with. Its activities, the sequence of operations that takes place in it, will be typical, nevertheless, of those in any architect's office. Although, therefore, I have chosen to describe a private office, much of my description will apply equally well to the daily round in a public office. An architect is an architect whoever employs him.

In this private office with a staff of twenty (the numbers may fluctuate from time to time as jobs begin and end) about twelve will probably be qualified architects, some of them experienced enough to take a lot of responsibility and regarded as regular members of the firm, some of them younger and more likely to move on in due course, to gain different experience in another office or set up on their own. There will probably be one or two younger still, who are learning the job by working in an office and preparing to qualify by taking the RIBA external examinations, and there may be two or three draughtsmen (or so-called technicians) who do not aspire to become architects in their own right and are all the more useful for having always concentrated on the job of producing working drawings and incorporating in them the details that only get decided on at the working-drawing stage.

Although I have used the word draughtsman only in connection with these relatively junior members of the staff, because that is what they are called, all the others are draughtsmen too in the sense that much of their day will be spent drawing: either producing the sequence of drawings by means of which the design for a building is evolved, or the working drawings prepared for the information and guidance of the contractor. The partners, too, will spend what proportion of their time they can at the drawing-board. I must emphasise again that an architect allows himself to be kept away from it at his peril; without a pencil in his hand he ceases to think like a real architect.

In addition to the staff enumerated above, there will be a couple of secretaries; one to act as personal secretary to the partners and one to do general typing and filing. There will be a telephonist who will probably also be the receptionist, there may also be a librarian, responsible for classifying and filing the great quantity and variety of information that comes into an architect's office—manufacturers' catalogues, revisions of building regulations, local authority planning notices, articles describing new developments in technical magazines and actual samples of materials and equipment: bricks, floor tiles, light fittings, door handles. The assistants in an office continually need to consult information or samples of this kind, and rely on having them systematically stored so that that they can easily be located. Finally there may be an office boy (or girl) to make tea and run errands, which will include constant journeys taking rolls of drawings to the printers.

It is unlikely that an office of this size can afford to employ the specialist staff to be found in a large office. This includes a business manager or accountant (the partners in a small office will have to do their own accounts) and a model-maker (much use is made nowadays of models, especially simply block models of balsa-wood, not so much to display to clients as to help visualise the form of a building and see how the parts relate when looked at from different directions). In a small office these working models will be made by assistants who have a talent for such things, and the more realistically finished models for showing to clients or sending to exhibitions will be put in the hands of professional model-makers.

A big office will also have its own printing machine with some-one to run it. Architects continually need drawings printed—that is, mechanically reproduced by one of several methods used, such as dye-line prints which come out as dark brown lines on white paper or blue-prints which come out as white lines on a dark blue background, when the original drawing on transparent linen or tracing paper is put into the printing machine. Several copies are needed, for example, of each set of working drawings: one for the contractor, one for the quantity surveyor, one for the heating engineer, one for the district surveyor of the local authority who has to check that bylaws have been obeyed, one for the architect's own use and one for filing as a future record. In a small office without its own printing machine, the negatives are sent out to the local printing office, though the architect's office probably has a small copying machine for reproducing documents, worked by the typist or office boy.

The cost of printing adds up to a large amount, but fortunately for architects the RIBA scale of fees allows them to pass some of their printing costs on to their clients. Printing can also cause delays. An architect's commonest excuse, when a contractor complains that work is being held up because drawings are overdue, is that he is waiting for them to come back from the printers.

The office I am describing will have a number of projects going on at the same time, but of course all at different stages. An office of this size might, at a given moment, be designing a fairly large school for the local education authority and preparing the working drawings for a housing scheme in a new town, already past the design stages. The partners might be making the first sketches for a new factory and discussing possible sites with a client who is considering building another factory. An extension to the local cottage hospital might also be at the working-drawing stage, a small office building nearing completion, along with the conversion of several adjoining shops in another town into one large one, a couple of private houses might be at different stages and a large Victorian house being converted into flats. One or two of the assistants might be helping one of the partners with the drawings for a competition for which he had entered and a junior assistant, with a flair for attractive draughtsmanship, might be occupying some of his time preparing drawings of some past office project to send to an exhibition or a water-colour perspective for a client to show to his board of directors.

The foregoing roughly indicates the load of work an office of this size could carry, and the two partners would be concerned with all of it, closely or remotely according to the stage it had reached. Because of this, their own time would be spent trying to give attention to a large number of matters at the same time, inside or outside the office. Only now and then, when a job was in the early stages, would one of the partners shut himself in his own office for several days at a stretch, concentrating on the design, trying to work out the relative merits of several different arrangements of the plan and spoiling any number of sheets of tracing paper while doing so.

By contrast, the assistants would spend nearly all their time on the same job until it was finished. A senior assistant would have been put in charge of the school and would be working out details of the design after agreeing its main lines with one of the partners, and another assistant would be helping him, making studies of different details and preparing preliminary drawings for the client's approval. Another senior assistant would be in charge of the housing scheme, and with a team of two or three others would be preparing the working drawings. Yet another would be working on the specification (which is the written description of the work to be done, and the nature and quality of the materials to be used, which goes to the contractor along with the drawings), and while he was doing so would be making repeated telephone calls to the quantity surveyor. In this case, since all the designing had already been done, the partners would not be involved except to be consulted if some decision had to be taken of a kind that needed their assent—or if there was some crisis, for example a message from the client that the money allocated to this particular housing project was being cut down (it sometimes happens even at so late a stage), and ways must be found of building it more cheaply.

The other jobs going forward in the office would similarly be in the hands of other assistants or groups of assistants, most of whose time would be spent at their drawing-boards since the partners would themselves undertake most of the outside work: attending meetings with clients (who tend to demand the presence of the architect himself even when the purpose of the meeting is to settle something an assistant could deal with), discussing site developments with the local planning officer, co-ordinating designs with heating and electrical engineers and visiting sites. Routine visits to inspect progress on sites where builidng work was going on might however be left to senior assistants. So would survey work.

An architect, besides making himself thoroughly familiar with a site before deciding how to make the best use of it—where to place a building and how to adapt its shape and planning to the lie of the land, from the point of view of aspect, slope, access and the existence of trees and other assets—will also have, at an early stage, to make an exact survey of it so as to have a record to work from of its exact dimensions and levels, the position of trees and the nature of the soil. Survey work is taught in the architectural schools. It needs experience, too, but unless any tricky problems arise it can usually be left to a fairly junior assistant. In the case of conversion work, an exact survey of the building to be converted will be needed, together with an examination of its structural condition which may need the experience of an expert.

The best way to give an impression of an architect's daily round will be perhaps to describe how one of the partners in the imaginary office I have been discussing might spend a typical day. After going through his correspondence first thing in the morning and dictating some letters to his secretary, he is almost ready for his first appointment outside, but before leaving he has a quick word with his partner to check on the day's programme of work and in case there are any urgent questions for them to settle. The senior assistant in charge of the school may also want a session with him to discuss the design and how it is working out. Then he is ready for his first meeting.

This is with the planning officer at county hall and is about one of the sites his industrialist client is considering for his factory. Its purpose is to find out what restrictions there are on the use of the site and what future plans there are for the neighbourhood, which might affect it: plans for new roads, perhaps, that would give it better—or less convenient—access. From county hall he goes to the site of the small office building to keep an appointment with the contractor. Here he has quite a number of things to do: inspect some plaster-work that on his last visit he had complained was uneven and that the contractor's foreman had promised to do again; decide on the colour some of the doors are to be painted on the basis of some samples the foreman has promised to have ready; discuss with the contractor himself a change in the roofing material, following a telephone call the day before warning him that there were delays in delivery of the material originally speci-fied, which would hold up completion of the building; hand in some drawings of last-minute joinery details which the contractor is urgently needing.

He takes the opportunity of looking over the building with the contractor, who himself takes the opportunity of reminding the architect that another payment is due to him. The architect there-upon makes a note that when he gets back to the office he must make out a certificate stating that enough work has been satis-factorily completed on the site to justify further payment, and send it to the client asking him to send the contractor a cheque.

The architect now has a quick lunch in a pub and then goes on to a manufacturer's showroom to have a look at a new range of light fittings he is thinking of using at the cottage hospital, and find out about colours and prices. He is told to his surprise, just as he is about to leave, that his secretary is on the telephone. She has remembered he was calling in there and wants to catch him about an urgent message that arrived at the office during the morning. This was about the shop-conversion job; one of the assistants in the office, visiting the site, had found the client (the owner of a chain of shops who had his headquarters in another town) visiting it too, and he was proposing all sorts of changes that it would be difficult, and extremely expensive, to make now that the job was half done. The assistant had thought the architect would want to come along and argue with him before he left; so he hurries along and, after a time-wasting display of tact and patience, persuades the client to abandon some of his new ideas and makes quite sure the client understands how much extra the others will cost.

He goes from there straight back to the office, taking the assis-tant with him in his car so that he need lose no time starting on the fresh drawings these changes require. He arrives there in mid-afternoon, having hoped for some hours at his drawing-board (he is due to explain his sketches for the second factory at a board meeting the following week, and still has a lot of work to do on them), only to find a message that a meeting of the new town housing corporation, for whom his housing scheme has been designed, is to take place in a couple of days and that they want him to attend and discuss various questions concerning landscaping and maintenance costs. He hopes this does not mean more last-minute changes—it might possibly mean, on the other hand, that they are planning to embark on another housing scheme and are thinking of giving him the job. He will have to come to the meeting armed with various estimates and figures, so he calls for all the papers that may help and sits down to work these out.

When he has finished the day has almost gone, but there is just time for a session over the drawing-board with another assistant who is working on one of the private houses but does not seem able to get the accommodation asked for fitted comfortably on to the site—or not without cutting down some trees that both architect and client are anxious to keep.

After a quick word with the assistant in charge of the hospital extension about the progress of the working drawings, and after signing his letters and making some notes about one or two urgent tasks to be seen to next day, he is free to leave the office, but he still has to decide between going to the monthly meeting of the local civic society of which he is an active member (he ought to go, because it is a cause that should be supported, though the agenda for this evening's meeting does not seem to have anything on it to which he can contribute much), and going to have a drink with a friend who wants to introduce him to an old army colleague who is going to be there with his wife. They sound rather a dull couple but, from a hint dropped by his friend, it seems as if there might be a job in the offing.

The foregoing gives some impression of a private architect's daily routine and that of the assistants who work for him. If, like 40 per cent of architects, he works in a *public* office his routine will not be very different. The same proportion of his time will be spent on the drawing-board, on working at estimates of cost and preparing specifications, on visiting sites and keeping an eye on the progress and quality of the work. The chief difference is that there will not be the same worry about finding clients and gaining their confidence—the client is the authority he works for—and that a large number of the necessary meetings will take place in other departments of the same office; consultations, for example, with the same authority's planning officer and its structural and heating and electrical engineers.

And the number of meetings will be larger because the architects or their senior assistants will have to explain and seek approval for their designs not only at personal meetings with their fellow officials—the education officers if they are designing schools, the legal officers if one of their jobs is a new law-court building and so on—but also at meetings of the elected councillors who are ultimately responsible: the county education committee, the borough housing committee and so on.

The public authority architect, too, is less of a jack-of-all-trades than a private architect because he has many specialists available for consultation—and expecting to be consulted. He must work with the authority's landscape architect instead of taking his own decisions about tree planting, and a number of matters that a private architect might decide differently on every job will be laid down for him by the accepted policy and practice of his authority.

None of the foregoing accounts of an architect's daily round include everything he has to spend his time on or take responsibility for; moreover he always has to be thinking ahead. If a client is likely to want a mural painting in his boardroom it will not do to wait till the building is nearly finished before looking round for a suitable artist. The architect must see that a decision is taken at an early stage so that he and the artist can work in consultation; and similarly with special decorations and fittings.

It may now be useful, as a way of filling the gaps in the above description of an architect's regular activities, to list the sequence of operations required to design and bring to completion a single building—operations that may be spread over less than a year or several years and are much the same whether the office from which they are conducted is a private or a public one.

First comes briefing by the client: his own account of what he wants. Sometimes this is precise; the client may be able to provide an exact schedule of accommodation. Far more often all he provides is an account of how his building is to be used, and it is for the architect to advise him about the kind of building that would best fulfil his needs. The architect is like a doctor making a diagnosis: bringing his experience and imagination to bear on a varied amount of information which he pieces together to make an intelligible picture and then translates into a course of action. He must show the client not only how he can get what he has asked for, but what he might have asked for if he had known it could be provided.

The client may have a site ready, which the architect can help him use to the best advantage, or he may need advice in choosing a site. When the site has been found and surveyed and all possible information about the client's requirements has been noted (including how much money he is prepared to spend), the architect gets down to the sketch plans and in due course shows them to the client, together with a rough estimate of cost—which is bound to be rough at this stage but is nevertheless of the greatest importance. If the architect is cautious and gives him a high price the client may be discouraged from going ahead; if the architect gives him an optimistically low price he may feel later on that he has been misled and his confidence in his architect is weakened. The architect can often give his client useful advice about cost; for example about when it is worth his while spending a larger sum initially in order to reduce maintenance costs later on. He will also try to persuade him that quality may be lost if, for commercial reasons, he insists on a building being rushed up too quickly, not giving the architect enough time to study the problem and work out the best solution.

Only when this has been done will the architect be ready to show his rough sketches to the client, and at this stage there may be long discussions about everything from finance to aesthetics and from roofing materials to under-floor heating. This is the stage at which it is important for the architect to make sure that the client understands exactly what he is getting and what he is committed to—otherwise there will be trouble later on—and this is the stage, too, when the architect experiences most frustration if he has to deal with a multiple client, and multiple clients are becoming more and more usual. They may take the form of a board of directors, the governors of a school, a local housing or education committee, a hospital board or a new town corporation, and it is always more difficult to satisfy a group than an individual and to get a firm decision from it. Experienced architects learn to sense, at their first meetings with a board or committee, which members are the ones whose views will ultimately carry weight and address their arguments to them.

At this stage, or before it, it is the architect's responsibility to make sure that all the regulations are obeyed: building bylaws, fire regulations and planning restrictions of all kinds; also to obtain on his client's behalf all the permissions required by an increasing number of government and local authorities. This may involve delays or even, if there is difficulty about getting official approval, a long series of inquiries and appeals; at the best there will be time-consuming discussions with planning and other officials. The bureaucratic complexities of architectural practice are among the things architects and their clients increasingly complain about.

When all these procedures have been gone through and the sketch-plans and cost-estimates at last approved by the client, and planning permission obtained from the local authority, the really busy time inside the office begins. A set of drawings must be prepared, plans of every floor-level (including probably separate plans showing the drainage system), sections and elevations, and drawings to a larger scale of anything that needs showing in more detail. The need is to provide in these drawings all the information about the building a contractor will need: full dimensions, the means of construction from the foundations to the roof, the materials to be used. A specification will be written describing nearly everything all over again in words, with the quality of materials and finishes clearly laid down.

The job will then be 'ready for tender'; that is, printed sets of the drawings and copies of the specification will be ready for sending to building contractors so that they can furnish estimates of cost. These will probably be contractors chosen by the architect because he thinks them suitable and after he has made sure they would like to take on the job and so will quote a realistic price. Or they may be contractors who have applied for particulars after the existence of the project has been advertised. This is customary in the case of local authority work. In the meantime other sets of drawings will have gone to the heating engineers and similar people, who have been consulted at appropriate stages while the building was being designed, so that they can work out where the pipes must go and the position of heating plant and radiators. The contractor will need to know all this because it will affect the work he has to do, but the cost of heating will not necessarily be part of his tender. It and other items may be separately tendered for, or a lump sum allocated to cover them. A separate set of drawings will be needed for each one of the sub-contractors who is thus estimating separately for some portion of the work.

After the drawings and specification have been sent off there will be a lull in the architect's office—as far as this particular job is concerned—until the tenders come in. They will be submitted by the contractors in sealed envelopes on an agreed date so that none shall know what his rivals are estimating. Opening the envelopes will be an alarming occasion for the architect; it will reveal to him whether the initial cost-estimate he gave his client is anywhere near the mark. If it turns out to have been far too low he will have the awkward task of telling this to the client, finding if he is prepared to spend more, and if not discussing with him how the cost can be cut down, perhaps by reducing the accommodation or using cheaper materials. But if the contractor's estimate is near his own he can feel proud of himself and only needs to get his client's approval of the exact sum estimated before the contract can be signed.

He may have some special reason for advising his client to appoint one of the contractors who has not put in the lowest estimate (for example if he thinks he will do so much the better job, from the point of view of quality of workmanship, that a slightly higher price will be worth paying), but normally the lowest tender gets the job. There are, as I have indicated already, other methods of appointing a contractor than getting competitive tenders, especially when the job is a technically advanced one. The architect may choose a contractor whose experience and expertise are best suited to the job, or has the most suitable resources in the way of labour and plant, and then, with the help of a quantity surveyor, negotiate a contract with him; that is, agree on a fair price. Nevertheless the competitive tender is still the commonest method.

For the contract, which is an agreement between the client and contractor, signed in the architect's presence, the standard RIBA form will probably be used. This is not only a legal agreement to construct the building for a certain sum of money within a certain time, but sets out at what intervals the money must be paid, what the client's and the contractor's rights and obligations are and what procedure is to be followed in case of dispute. The contract having been signed, work can start on the site, and from now on most of the architect's work will be supervision, though he will still have to provide many drawings showing details that had not been decided at an earlier stage, take many decisions about materials and fittings and keep in touch with the work of specialists like heating engineers.

If the job is a large one he will probably appoint a clerk of works. The latter is the client's representative on the site and has an office there from which he keeps track of the progress of the building, makes sure materials are of the kind and quality specified and watches that workmanship is up to standard. But even if there is a clerk of works, the architect or one of his assistants must regularly visit the site, supervise quality, check progress and deal with problems that arise on the spot. The architect is the man ultimately responsible. To make sure everything goes smoothly he will probably make out a 'time and progress schedule', a chart showing the date when every stage of the work should be completed and when drawings and decisions must be made, to which he and his assistants will constantly refer.

He must also watch out for 'extras'—work ordered from the contractor as an afterthought, either by him or his client, and therefore not on the original drawings. The architect tries to avoid these; they add to the expense and may mount up to a large sum, which the client will resent. At the very least he must make sure the client realises what extra costs he is incurring, and does not give orders to the contractor without his knowledge.

With or without problems, delays, disputes and crises of confidence all round, the building will eventually be completed and formally handed over by the contractor to the client. The architect's first action will then probably be to have photographs taken, before the client moves in and starts, in the architect's view, spoiling it by rearranging the furniture and having notices put up using lettering the architect did not choose and does not like. The architect wants photographs for his own record and to send to architectural magazines.

After completion of the building there is a period—usually six months—during which the contractor is responsible for defects that may occur and during which he expects to have to deal with minor teething troubles. Then the final instalment of his money is paid to him. The architect is by now fairly sure that nothing serious has gone wrong. He is responsible, along with the contractor, if something should occur as alarming as a structural collapse, and wholly responsible if it is shown that this has been due to his design; so, anyhow with a large job, he will have taken out an insurance policy covering him against claims for negligence.

Normally, however, the architect's job, like the contractor's, is officially at an end when the building has been handed over, but he is unlikely to be allowed to consider it so for quite a while. Clients tend to think of their architect as being at their disposal to deal with the most trivial occurrences, and even more so the client's employees. The matron at the cottage hospital will send messages to his office about dripping taps for weeks after the extension has been finished, and the manager of the shops will expect him to call round personally every time the new central heating plant needs adjusting.

That is the price an architect pays for being in so many ways a jack-of-all-trades, and he must be satisfied with debiting his wasted time to the cause of establishing good relations all round. His aim, naturally, is to finish with a client wholly satisfied with his building. The architect himself is unlikely to be satisfied. He is learning all the time, and when he thinks about a building he has just completed he probably wishes he had it to do all over again so that he could design it quite differently.

CHAPTER EIGHT

A Look Ahead

The demand for architects and their services is not likely to diminish in the foreseeable future (it has been calculated that the number of new buildings required during the next thirty years will equal the total number of buildings of whatever age at present standing); but the architect's exact role will have to be adjusted to meet a number of changes that have already begun to threaten his position.

These are of different kinds. One, for example, arises from attempts to exploit the need for his services commercially but at the same time escape the restrictions imposed by his professional independence. It is known as the 'package deal', a phenomenon that has only appeared during the past ten years, much to the architectural profession's alarm. The term means that the prospective client—the industrialist, say, who is planning to build a new factory or head office—is offered, as part of the same package, all the services he will require: help in finding a site, a design for the building to go on it, the services of specialists like structural and heating engineers and the construction and supervision of the building itself.

This has an obvious appeal. When once he has put himself in the hands of the company offering this package (probably a contracting firm, or, more likely, a subsidiary company set up by a contracting firm for this purpose) he is saved any more trouble, and he possibly saves money because the company, providing everything as part of the same operation can save on overheads and offer him a cheaper job—or what appears to be a cheaper job because he has to pay no separate architect's or consultant's fees and has no way of calculating to what extent the total sum he is paying may have been increased to allow for these.

In practice it will almost certainly have been increased, because the company will have to employ architects, or staff with architectural qualifications, to make the design and prepare the drawings; so the only savings will be administrative ones, plus the difference between the amount an architect would charge in fees and the amount the company pays in salaries to its perhaps less well qualified architect-employees. In return for whatever saving there is, the client foregoes the independent advice he would have got from an architect. Instead of having an architect watching his interests, he is wholly in the hands of a company whose only reason for giving him a fair deal is likely to be the hope of more building work in the future.

Described like that it sounds a poor bargain, but the package deal is showing signs of establishing itself, at least for some types of building. It does save the busy client trouble, but the main reason for its success must be the client's unawareness of the value of an architect and the disinterested service he is trained to give. If architects do not want their position gradually undermined, they will have to show that the package deal is not the way to get the best results. On aesthetic grounds this is easily demonstrated. The package deal has so far produced very commonplace buildings, no doubt because those responsible for designing them, the architects who have taken up employment in these contracting companies, are capable of nothing better; it is not a job likely to attract a top-level designer because in this sort of operation good design standards are given a low priority.

On grounds of efficiency and economy the difference is not so easy to establish; independent architects must prove, through their own buildings, that they can offer a better deal. They and the institutions that represent them must demonstrate to the client the value of a disinterested study of his needs and of the alternatives he should be considering; also the value of designs made specially for him as distinct from adaptations of some standard product. They must show the client how much he gains by his interests being put first when they do not happen to coincide with those of the contractor, who is after all primarily concerned with financial profits.

It is important for the architect to preserve his independence, not only for the sake of the duty he owes his client but for the sake of the duty he owes to society, and especially to the environment he is helping to shape. If the architect does not bear the public interest in mind no one else will—certainly not the package-deal contractor; in fact one definition of the architect's professional role is that he has to endeavour to contrive that his client's wants shall coincide with the public needs. The failure to do this, because he is not capable or does not care, is at the root of many of our environmental failures and justifies our putting some of the blame for them on the architect. An architect who is, in effect, a prisoner of the contracting or property development industry is in no position to keep the balance between new development and the existing environment; neither to play his proper role as a conservationist nor to ensure that new developments improve the environment.

The use of the package deal and similar devices has been encouraged by new technical developments and especially the increased use of industrially produced building components. These tend to merge the design and the construction processes and obscure the role the architect traditionally plays. But it is the same techniques—or, rather, the thoughtless use of them—that produce most of the buildings that are now doing so much harm to the environment, and the architect's participation at every stage becomes all the more important in order to ensure that these techniques are not used simply because they are handier and cheaper and that their effect on the environment is watched.

I have paid a lot of attention to the package deal because it is not only an economic device but a symptom of the ways architects have been getting out of touch with developments characteristic of our time, of which they should remain in command, instead of allowing themselves to become the victims. Those who make use of the package deal are, in effect, classifying the architect as someone who no longer has a vital part to play in the building process. It is therefore not enough for him to go on the defensive and plead for a return to the situation when his authority and status were unquestioned. In many case there never was such a situation; even in the last century, when the prestige of the celebrity architect was at its height, he was responsible for only a minority of outstanding buildings, and the ordinary buildings—the housing, the factories and workshops—which transformed and urbanised the landscape and whose environmental deficiencies we are still suffering from today, were put up without his help.

The business of architecture is changing, and architects and their professional organisations must be prepared to change with it. The latter are dimly aware of this—hence all the recent fuss in Britain about proper representation of the salaried architect and about the status of the technician—but too many architects, perhaps because of notions induced in them when they were students, still hanker after a nineteenth-century image. Such an image is incompatible with many new developments, technical and administrative, of which the package deal is only one. Another is the increasing part being played in building by ready-made components and proprietary structural systems, in Britain, in other industrialised countries and even more in America, as a result of which the architect could easily be forced into the position of someone who merely chooses parts available from factories and assembles and dresses them up in an attractive way—becoming a kind of visual public-relations man. If he accepts this role he is in danger of losing control of the quality of the finished product; for example many of the tall blocks of flats recently built in our towns and cities, which we now find disfiguring to the environment and poorly suited to family life, are there not because an architect has decided that they provide the best answer to a problem but because the proprietors of the system by which they are constructed have persuaded the local authority to adopt it as being cheaper or quicker to build with. The authority's architect has either not been consulted or has preferred to earn credit with his employers by helping them produce impressive housing figures to worrying about good architecture. In either case he has lost control of the final result, which amounts to dereliction of duty on the part of a professional man.

The ready-made products out of which many modern buildings are put together, and on which their quality and character largely depends, were not designed by architects; so they find many decisions that should be theirs taken before they start. Architects must now find some way of regaining control of the material they use, either by involving themselves more closely in the industries where standards are set and decisions—especially aesthetic decisions—taken, or by some form of collaboration between themselves and the present wide variety of industrial designers, engineers, manufacturers and contractors, so that all can contribute their particular skills at the stage at which they are needed.

The possibilities in this direction are suggested by Britain's achievements in school building after the last war. So great was the need for new schools, especially in the counties round London where the population was expanding fastest—a need created by the reform of education as well as by the stoppage of school building caused by the war—that methods had to be found of building new schools more quickly and economically than was possible by traditional methods. The Hertfordshire county architect, with the encouragement of the education officer, got together with various manufacturers of building components and their engineers, and between them they devised a system of building schools out of standard interchangeable parts, the most important of which were light steel columns and beams and prefabricated wall-panels of various materials.

These parts were mass produced and stored in depots in different parts of the county, from which they could be drawn as needed, for the many schools that were built simultaneously. Since the parts were relatively small and could be assembled in any way, each school could be of different design to suit the site and its orientation and the accommodation required. Most important of all, because these interchangeable parts and the economical building system they made possible had been designed with architects in control, the finished buildings were satisfactory works of architecture, in fact were in many ways an improvement on earlier types of school.

The Hertfordshire experiment had a wide influence. The Ministry of Education took it up and developed it further, again under the control of its own architects, and later the official architects in other counties (or groups of counties in localities where the demand for schools was not big enough to justify such a highly industrialised method) developed similar and even more ambitious systems—permitting the use, for example, of multi-storey buildings—suited to their needs. The most successful of these systems, known as 'Clasp', has proved very useful and adaptable and has become a British export to other countries.

The foregoing is only one example of how the architect, in collaboration with others, can help to overcome the problems set by industrialisation and prefabrication. And the building industry must contribute a greater share. At present it is poorly organised, with too many small firms capable of doing only traditional kinds of work and with bad labour relations in the bigger firms. And because of the weighty and immovable nature of most building materials it does not have to compete with better designed or better made products imported from abroad, and so has little incentive to improve. The building industry spends barely one-fifth of 1 per cent of its total expenditure on research and the development of new products, whereas manufacturing industry spends 4 per cent.

The use of new techniques must be improved because they are here to stay. This is not only because we cannot turn our backs on what our own age has invented—no past generation has ever built less skilfully and economically than it knew how—but because the pressing problems of the underdeveloped world, the shortage of housing, schools and other essential types of building, can only be solved, because of its vast extent, by the use of these techniques. The export of prefabricated components, specially designed for such purposes, and of the know-how required to make the best use of them, is one of the benefits the industrialised countries can offer to the rest of the world. In fact awareness among architects and their institutions of the needs of other parts of the world is one of the encouraging new developments of recent years.

There are many signs of growing internationalism within the profession. They include exchanges of teachers and students; agreements on the international standardisation of the signs and symbols used on architects' drawings (architects were among the first people in Britain to begin the switch from feet and inches to metres and centimetres); and the recent activities of the International Union of Architects, an organisation founded after the last war and based in Paris, to whose meetings and congresses Britain, through the RIBA, has always sent strong delegations. The East European countries play an active part in the work of the IUA, and a remarkable sign of its unifying potentialities is that its meetings have been almost the only international occasions when East and West Germany have been represented by joint delegations.

International co-operation of a more positive and practical kind is likely to result from Britain's membership of the European Economic Community. Discussions about the mutual recognition in the different countries of each other's professional qualfications, which would allow architects in one of the member countries to practise in the others, have been going on for ten years, with Britain taking part in advance of her joining the Community. These discussions have, however, run into difficulties, resulting both from different professional traditions and different methods of work (see Appendix 6). In Germany, Italy and Belgium, for example, less distinction is made than in Britain between architects and engineers. In Germany there is also the complication of the near-autonomy, in matters of professional regulation, of the regional administrations (*länder*) and there is no uniformity among them, and in Germany too, and in some of the other EEC countries, a two-tier profession is already established; that is, a profession including both fully qualified architects and a separate class of technicians on the lines sometimes advocated for Britain— see Chapter 2 of this book. In some EEC countries salaried assistants are not allowed to call themselves architects, a restriction which, if introduced into Britain, would disqualify half the profession.

Another difficulty is that the Liaison Committee of Architects of the Common Market, the committee that has been holding these discussions, has suggested that any mutual recognition of degrees or diplomas should be based simply on the length of the school course which has led to the diploma being granted. This would take no account of the *quality* of the course and therefore of the standard demanded from those completing it. The standard required in some Continental schools of architecture is well below that of the recognised British schools, and it is obviously undesirable that permission to practise in Britain should be given to less well qualified European architects and to architects with a less strict code of professional ethics. Nor should Europe be allowed to strengthen once again in Britain the notion of the celebrity architect who only makes sketches for his inferiors to carry out. Rather should Britain export her newly developed emphasis on architecture as a social service.

Still another difficulty is that in Britain the institutions that govern the architectural profession, and the universities where most architects are trained, are almost wholly independent of the government, whereas in other EEC countries they are subject to direct government control. Nevertheless not all the virtues are on the British side of the Channel, and the problems that have delayed the mutual recognition of architects' qualifications must and will eventually be solved, though it is likely that for some years to come the differences in building regulations and methods of work will make it necessary for an architect from a different country to associate himself with a local architect. The best start might be more students studying and working in other countries.

Britain can be said, many years ago, to have initiated the process of expanding the administration and teaching of architecture into an international network through the historical accident, already referred to, whereby the qualifications first recognised in all the Commonwealth countries were those of the RIBA, and the fact that before these countries had their own architectural schools most of their young architects came to Britain for their training. An important extension of this practice was the establishment, by the AA school in London soon after the last war, of a post-graduate School of Tropical Architecture—the only one of its kind. There young architects from many parts of Asia, Africa, the Caribbean and Latin America came to study the special problems, and exchange experience, of building for tropical climates and especially for people who had still to develop their own research and industrial facilities. The school is now part of the School of Environmental Studies at University College, London.

In countries all over the world there are new developments, in addition to the increase of industrialisation, that are changing not only the architect's professional and social responsibilities but the way he sets about his job. One is the development, in certain types of building, of highly complex services in addition to the usual water, gas and electricity: air-conditioning, controlled heating, internal communications (including closed-circuit television) and the like, to such a degree that the economical layout of these services, rather than the structural skeleton, becomes the framework, as it were, on which the building is planned. This makes it all the more necessary for the architect to work as one of a team, alongside the specialist engineers who plan these services.

Another development is the increased need for flexible space, again because of the complexity of the activities for which certain types of building have to be designed. The exact planning of buildings for a particular function is being replaced by the provision of space for adaptable use. Moreover certain types of building, like hospitals and science laboratories, tend soon to become obsolete because of changes in medical treatment and in the techniques and subjects of research. This makes flexibility a great convenience, and may lead to a greater demand for temporary structures. Buildings made of prefabricated parts can much more easily be dismantled and renewed as needed, and we may gradually come to accept the idea that a building need not have the quality of permanence that we have always associated with the art of architecture.

It should, however, be remembered that we should lose as much as we gained if we took so much advantage of the possibility of building for temporary use as to discard the solidity of our built environment. We must not deprive our buildings of their role of giving historical continuity to cities and a sense of stability to our surroundings. For continuity and stability are psychologically, as we are now coming to recognise, of the utmost importance. They are closely linked, for example, with one of our most worrying modern problems: the decline in security in spite of greater affluence. Violence is largely a symptom of frustration, and one of the causes of frustration is deficiencies in the environment: bad housing, exhausting journeys to work, the failure of an over-urbanised environment to give access to a full and varied life, and its failure to give everyone a sense of belonging to, and participating in, a stable community. Places preserving their own identity is one of the things that ensures a stable community.

In trying to solve these problems society must control technology so that it becomes our servant and not our master, and in this process architects must play a leading part. It is easy for architects to be so seduced by the fascination of experimenting with new materials and techniques as to put the means before the ends. If they persist in doing so they will find themselves in a trap from which they cannot escape; the prisoners, for example, of industrial systems we think we are using but are really using us. Uncritical acceptance of new technologies can reduce the element of choice, and freedom of choice—freedom to employ whatever techniques and materials, new or old, best suit the job in hand— is something the architect, on behalf of the community, must struggle to preserve.

A situation peculiar to our time is that technically there is almost nothing we cannot do. In earlier times architects were continually searching for new techniques in order to achieve what they had never achieved before—such as cover larger spaces or construct a greater number of storeys—but now they are searching instead for the right use, socially and humanly as well as structurally, for the infinite number of new techniques at their disposal, which are embracing a wider range of sciences than ever before. There are, to give but one instance, computerised methods of ascertaining needs by analysing things like changes in family structure and rates of traffic flow, which ought, in theory, to enable our varied building techniques to be far more accurately applied to the solution of real problems. Hit or miss should be a method of the past.

Provided the architect learns to collaborate constructively with the scientists, engineers, sociologists and administrators whose expertise he must both share and contribute to, he can play a large part in coping with the environmental consequences of all the social changes that have lately taken place. Among these are our greater mobility (resulting from the ubiquitous motor car which, however, as a means of social contact threatens to be self-defeating), the greater density of population, an increasing proportion of old people and a different use of the longer hours of leisure that the mechanisation of labour promises to provide.

That is why our present emphasis on the environment is much more than a fashionable catchword. The change we face today is that our highly technological, highly urbanised, society has suddenly found that the quality of its environment cannot any longer be left to chance. The architect's old preoccupations with the deployment of space, and with style and technique in terms of individual buildings, have come to mean less and less if these buildings are not playing their proper part in the total scene; and the same qualities of control and co-ordination, the same ability to transform chance into design, that the architect has always applied to buildings, are now needed in the wider field of the environment.

The more far-sighted architects are searching—as they have been doing since the time of William Morris—for a new integration between the practical and the creative aspects of existence, which we have lately found to our concern tend to separate themselves into different and even opposing cultures. Architecture, since it contains an element of both, is ideally qualified to serve as a bridge, linking those increasingly divergent activities, the sciences and the arts.

But contemporary architecture, as it has developed in recent years, has failed to show itself capable of fulfilling this role. I have already expressed the opinion that the exaggerated anxiety to preserve old buildings just because they are old, shown by many educated people, is at least partly due to mistrust of what architects will put in their place. There is at the moment, in fact, a crisis of confidence between the architect and his public, the result of an unfortunate combination of circumstances, some of which I have hinted at in earlier chapters.

These are not all the fault of the architect, who has nearly as much right to be critical of the public as the public of him. A good and responsible standard of architecture depends on a well informed public opinion supporting it, yet the public continually shows itself both ignorant of, and uninterested in learning about, architecture. School children are taught nothing about it, although modern developments in the other arts—music, poetry, painting and sculpture—are at the very least drawn to their attention. If they are told anything about architecture, it is only about its past. As a result of this ignorance, nearly half a century after the revitalisation of architecture was made possible by the acceptance and the aesthetic exploitation of modern ideas and techniques, many people still have an instinctive hankering after buildings that echo one of the historic styles; or at best a resistance to studying and trying to understand why buildings are now different and what modern architects are aiming at. Yet one would not expect to appreciate poetry in a language one had not learnt.

One cannot altogether blame the man in the street if his sensibilities have been blunted by the brashness and confusion he sees all round him, and yet until knowledge and understanding of the architecture of our own day is considered part of the well educated man's equipment, as are modern poetry, music and art, architects will continue to work in a vacuum and everyone else will regard it as a mystery beyond his comprehension. I have already stressed the importance to architecture of more discriminating clients, and of more public participation in the researches into needs and how they can be fulfilled which architects undertake on the public's behalf. I might also have stressed, although this is not the place to embark on discussions of political economy, that governments who control the economy cannot escape some share of the blame when architecture seems to get its priorities wrong; for example when the public sector of the nation's building programme, which tries to answer long-term social requirements, has to compete for the capital it needs, and for its proper share of the available labour and materials, with private enterprises only concerned with making a quick profit. Until all these matters are more sensibly managed, the public has little right to complain about architects' shortcomings.

Except the shortcomings of incompetent architects, for which there is no excuse. By these I mean not only architects who are technically inefficient; whose roofs leak or in whose buildings you can hear everything that happens in the next room. I mean architects who are visually illiterate, have no sense of proportion or colour or harmonious design, who produce instead a meaningless assembly of clichés. Architects should remember, moreover, that the self-indulgent pursuit of novelty, of which too many of them are guilty, is one of the things that prevent the public from seeing modern architecture as normal and acceptable. If every new building is different, how can a recognisable contemporary idiom become established?

Nearly as bad as these obtrusive seekers after novelty are the architects who seem to imagine that the purpose of building is to erect a monument to themselves, and who therefore put the achievement of a striking result before anything else. They fail to recognise that the proper definition of a well designed building, in nine cases out of ten, is a building that fits so unobtrusively into its environment that its impact goes unnoticed. As I have emphasised already and must emphasise again, the architect owes a duty to the community as well as to himself and to the individual who employs him. It is because the practice of architecture impinges on the life of the community at so many points that, in spite of its present-day failures and deficiencies, it remains one of the most worthwhile professions as well as the most fascinating of the arts.

Appendices

Number of architects per head of population in different countries, based on a survey made in 1965 (no later figures available):

Britain	one architect to every	3,118 people
West Germany	,, ,, ,, ,,	1,300 ,,
Denmark	,, ,, ,, ,,	1,960 ,,
USA	,, ,, ,, ,,	7,616 ,,
Italy	,, ,, ,, ,,	9,250 ,,
Japan	,, ,, ,, ,,	76,404 ,,

(The figures for Germany include architect-engineers.)

In the less developed countries, such as those in Asia, Africa and Latin America, the number of architects is very much smaller, for example (only approximate figures are available in this case):

India	one architect to every	290,000 people
Ghana	,, ,, ,, ,,	154,000 ,,
Algeria	,, ,, ,, ,,	96,000 ,,
Colombia	,, ,, ,, ,,	75,000 ,,
Mexico	,, ,, ,, ,,	22,000 ,,

Distribution of British architects (1970) in different types of employment, given as a percentage of the total number of architects:

Local government		27·3
county councils	10·7	
county boroughs	8·5	
county districts	5·8	
new towns	2·3	
Central government		11·9
central government proper	7·2	
national boards and public corporations	4·7	
Private practice		48·9
principals	29·6	
assistants	19·3	
Teaching		3·3
Other		8·6
contracting firms	2·0	
commerce and industry	4·9	
miscellaneous	1·7	
Total		100

APPENDIX 3

Earnings by age in different branches of the architectural profession in Britain. The figures show average earnings in 1972, expressed in pounds per annum:

		age in 1970		
type of employment	under 35	35–44	45 & over	all ages
Local government	3,144	3,705	3,795	3,597
Central government	3,125	4,541	4,567	4,343
Private practice	2,705	3,944	4,560	3,764
Teaching	3,300	3,833	4,167	3,819
Other	3,271	4,367	4,217	4,132
All types	2,757	3,935	4,180	3,793

APPENDIX 4

Schools of architecture in Britain with a 5-year or 6-year full-time course leading to exemption from the RIBA final examination:

		Number of Students	
		full-time under-graduate	post-graduate or research
Aberdeen	Robert Gordon's Institute of Technology	200	16
Bath	University of Bath	104	
Belfast	The Queen's University	165	9
Birmingham	Polytechnic	188	
Brighton	Polytechnic	160	
Bristol	University of Bristol	170	
Cambridge	University of Cambridge	188	28
Canterbury	College of Art	123	
Cardiff	University of Wales (Institute of Science and Technology)	219	
Dundee	Duncan of Jordanstone College of Art	190	
Edinburgh	Heriot-Watt University	200	20
	University of Edinburgh	150	30
Glasgow	University of Strathclyde	225	
Hull	Regional College of Art	60	
Kingston-upon-Thames	Kingston Polytechnic	230	
Leeds	Polytechnic	210	
Leicester	Polytechnic	230	
Liverpool	University of Liverpool	230	
London	Architectural Association	420	52
	Central London Polytechnic	225	
	North London Polytechnic	186	
	Polytechnic of the South Bank	145	

		Number of Students	
		full-time under- graduate	*post- graduate or research*
	Thames Polytechnic	144	
	University College, University of London (School of Environmental Studies)	203	
Manchester	Polytechnic	125	
	University of Manchester	196	
Newcastle	University of Newcastle-upon-Tyne	180	
Nottingham	University of Nottingham	108	
Oxford	Polytechnic	280	
Portsmouth	Polytechnic	200	
Sheffield	University of Sheffield	200	

APPENDIX 5
British Institutions and Organisations

Royal Institute of British Architects, 66 Portland Place, London W1. The governing body of the profession (founded 1834), controlling the architect's ethics and his fees as well as architectural education. Compiles and issues statistics about the profession and conducts research into its activities (eg an illuminating survey 'The Architect and his Office' published in 1962). Organises meetings, lectures and exhibitions. Has one of the best architectural libraries in the world, and a collection of architectural drawings in another building: 21 Portman Square (alongside the Coutauld Institute). Has several regional branches (though its main activities take place in London—a fact much criticised by members elsewhere) and wide connections throughout the Commonwealth, since many Commonwealth architects rely on RIBA qualifications.

Royal Incorporation of Architects in Scotland, 15 Rutland Square, Edinburgh. The Scottish equivalent of the RIBA, though without the same resources and bureaucratic structure and therefore more resembling the academic professional institution the RIBA once was.

Architectural Association, 36 Bedford Square, London WC1. A club and meeting place for London architects, founded in 1847 to promote better education, and still mainly concerned with this since it controls the oldest and largest architectural school. Its most useful role is to keep students and practising architects in touch with each other.

Institute of Advanced Architectural Studies, King's Manor, York. Founded in 1953 by the York Academic Trust and now attached to the University of York. An enterprising body chiefly concerned with running specialised post-graduate courses; also a diploma course, occupying one year, on conservation.

National Buildings Record, 10 Great College Street, London SW1. A government organisation, set up during the war when many notable buildings were being destroyed, to assemble photographic and other records of important buildings. Now has over half a million photographs, geographically arranged.

Society for the Protection of Ancient Buildings, 55 Great Ormond Street, London WC1. A propaganda body which also offers technical advice on repair and restoration. There are other bodies devoted to the safeguarding of buildings of special periods: the *Georgian Group* (2 Chester Street, London SW1); the *Victorian Society* (29 Exhibition Road, London, SW7).

Civic Trust, 17 Carlton House Terrace, London, SW1. Founded 1957 with the aim of arresting the deterioration of the environment and encouraging higher standards of civic design. Mainly a propaganda body (through films, publications, awards, exhibitions and the promotion of local improvement schemes), but also co-ordinates the work of, and provides expert advice to, the many civic and amenity societies established throughout Britain.

APPENDIX 6
The Profession in the EEC Countries

	population in millions	number of architects	membership of the largest professional institution	number of full-time schools of architecture
Belgium*	9·7	5,900	4,000	18
Britain*	55·0	22,000	19,000	31
Denmark	4·9	2,500	2,000	2
Eire	3·0	1,400	700	2
France*	51·0	8,500	2,000	21
West Germany*	62·0	60,000	4,500	no figure available
Italy*	54·0	9,000	no figure available	10
Luxembourg*	0·35	25	no figure available	none
Netherlands	13·0	4,500	1,200	10

* In these countries architects are compulsorily registered. The number of architects given for Belgium and West Germany includes engineer-architects, and the number for Eire includes surveyors. In the case of Britain, the membership of the largest professional institution (the RIBA) includes about 5,000 overseas members, mostly in the British Commonwealth. Figures are by courtesy of the *RIBA Journal*.

Bibliography

BOOKS

Architecture and Landscape Architecture (HM Stationery Office, 1972). One of the useful series of pamphlets issued under the general title 'Choice of Careers' by the Central Youth Employment Executive.

Brett, Lionel. *Parameters and Images* (Weidenfeld & Nicolson, 1970). Unusually well written appraisal of the problems that face architecture today and of how they shoud be met, especially how architects should approach the various crises facing the big city and the threatened environment.

Fleming, John; Honour, Hugh and Pevsner, Nikolaus. *Penguin Dictionary of Architecture* (1966). Paper-back, illustrated by drawings, with clear definitions of all kinds of architectural terms though with a bias towards the historical.

Kaye, Barrington. *The Development of the Architectural Profession in Britain* (Allen & Unwin, 1960). A historical and sociological survey: dull but thorough.

Layton, Elizabeth. *Report on the Practical Training of Architects.* (RIBA, 1962). A short but useful summary, though now a little out of date chiefly because some of its recommendations, especially those concerned with practical experience during training, have been acted upon.

Richards, J. M. *An Introduction to Modern Architecture* (Penguin Books). First published in 1940 to explain the principles of modern architecture, then relatively new to Britain, and the background out of which it had emerged. It has been several times revised and is still relevant as a general account.

Senior, Derek. *Your Architect* (Hodder & Stoughton, 1964). An excellent non-technical account of what kind of professional man an architect is, what he does and how he sets about it. Written, however, on behalf of the RIBA and therefore not at all critical of architects' work.

Smith, D. L. *How to Find Out in Architecture and Building* (Pergamon Press, 1967). A compact reference book, listing and describing the available sources of information: books, periodicals, libraries and institutions.

Spyer, Geoffrey. *Architect and Community* (Peter Owen, 1971). A study by a practising architect of recent developments in building and planning, their legislative background and their social implications.

The Architect and His Office (RIBA, 1962). It is creditable that the RIBA should have compiled and published this frank exposition of the architect's problems and shortcomings as an administrator. A similar critical analysis of the results of his work as a designer would be an even braver undertaking.

PERIODICALS

The Architectural Review. Monthly, published by the Architectural Press, 9 Queen Anne's Gate, London SW1. Covers not only architecture, historical and modern, but planning, landscape, interior design, townscape (a term popularised by the magazine) and to some extent the fine arts. Edited nearly as much for the interested non-architect as for the professional man. High standard of layout and illustration.

The Architects' Journal. Weekly, also published by the Architectural Press. The principal magazine for the practising architect, dealing with professional politics and providing news, technical information and illustrations of new buildings, with their planning, structure and costs fully analysed.

Journal of the Royal Institute of British Architects. Monthly, issued free to members. More than a record of the institute's doings as it comments on current problems and policies and publishes articles and book reviews.

Index

A- and O-level subjects required, 100

Accounting, 108; *see also* office overheads

Acoustics, 26

Adam, Robert and brother James, 31

Aesthetics, 20–1, 59, 78, 115, 122, 125

Age at which normally qualified, 70

Air conditioning, 26, 129

Airlines, architects serving with, 37

Alterations, fees for, 89

Ambition, 72

American Institute of Architects, 54

Analyst of social needs, architect as, 21

Anonymity in competitions, 52

Appeals in planning, 23

Arbitrations, 55, 59

Architects: and engineers, the similarity between, 15–19, 25–6; as planners, 19–20; as visionaries, 16; at the top, do they administer rather than design?, 34; average age of, tendency to rise, 70; average earnings of, 85–8, 136; building-user relations, 41–2; collaborators with, 13–29; debarred from accepting commission from contractors and tradesmen, 55; dislike of writing, 71; distribution of, by job classification (*table*), 136; duties from day to day, 105–20; duties of, in earlier times, 13–15; extent of liability, 119; freelance, the problem of regular work-flow, 46 (*see also* work-flow, irregularity in); have no news value, 91; how to choose good, 44–9; landscape, 26–7, 78, 110; leisure time of, 69–70; need to know in detail how other people function so as to

Architects—*cont'd.*

design efficiently, 20; normal sporting likes of, 70; numbers of per head of population (*table*), 135; own private houses, 68–9; panels of, advising local planners, 24; perform a social service, 30; prohibition of, as certain company directors, 55; protected profession under Architects' Registration Act (1931), 53; Registration Council Act (1938), 53–4, 101; second rate, still a superfluity of, 47–8, 57; see architecture all their waking hours, 67–8; see through whole project from beginning to end, 38–9; sometimes subservient to untrained planners, 23–4; supply of, not out-running demand, 71, 73, 84, 121; well established cannot charge greater fees, 46; what kind of persons are they?, 63–75; women as, 63–4

Architectural: Association School, (London: 1847), 93, 96; boards of registration (US—one for each State), 54; lettering, 95; revolution (1920s), 17; schools, 18, 21, 30–1, 35, 53, 57, 93–6, (*list of*) 137–8; technicians, 40–1, 107

Architecture, a growing and increasing profession, 70–1; as a lasting art, 43; consultancy in, 21, 79; need to show off full capabilities of, 44–5; not a get-rich-quick profession, 84; still not regarded as a teaching subject in education, 48; studying, 93–104

ARIBA, 83–4, 98

Articles, 93–4

Assessors in competitions, 51–2

Associates, *see* ARIBA

Awards, 42

Banking, architects serving, 37

Bibliography, 141–3

Birmingham School of Architecture, 97

Blueprints, 108

Board of Architectural Education (RIBA's), 101

Bridges, 15–16

Briefs for competitions, 52

British Rail, architects serving, 37

Brunel, Sir Marc Isambard and son, Isambard Kingdom, 16

Building contract, standard form of, 55, 118

Burlington, Earl of, 14

Business acumen, need for, 65–6

Bylaws, 28, 116

Cabinet-makers, 13

Capacity, the need to have work to maximum, 44; *see also* workflow, irregularity in

Carpenters, 13

Carvers, 13

Cathedrals, 15, 27, 36

Central Electricity Generating Board, architects serving, 37

Chambers, Sir William, 31

Chartered Architect, use of title, 53

Churches, 15, 20

Cinemas, 20, 27

Civic Amenities Act (1967), 61

Civil engineers, 15

'Clasp' system, 126

Clerks of Works, 13, 118

Clients, discussing fees with, 90; wants must also coincide with public needs, 123

Coal Board, architects serving, 37

Code of Professional Conduct, 14, 55, 88

Colour slides, 69; *see also* photographing

Commercial offices, speculative, 37

Commissioned work, 37, 42

Common Market, opportunities in, 52, 127–8, 129, 140

Commonwealth, architects from, 54

Competitions, 49–53

Completion dates, importance of, 77

Computers, 41, 82

Concrete, 15

Conditions of Engagement and Scale of Professional Charges (RIBA pamphlet), 90

Consultancy, 21, 79

Contracts, 55, 118

Conversions, fees for, 89

Copying machine, 108

Costing projects, 27–8, 52, 77

Criticism, opportunity for and usefulness of, 42–3

Dates of completion, importance of, 77

Day's work, outline of a typical, 111–13

Dead men, trading on the reputation of, 82

Department of Environment, 58

Design drawings, 39, 41, 66

Designing at the drawing board, 39, 41

Discussion between architects, why it is so often confused, 71

Docks, 14, 16

Drainage, 116

Draughtsman, 14, 38–40, 80–1, 107; *see also* architectural technicians

Drawings in design, 39, 41, 65–6

Ducts, pipes and cables, 26

Duties, day to day, 105–20

Dye-line prints, 108

Earnings, average, 85–8, 136

EEC, *see* Common Market

Elections to RIBA Council, 57

Electrical engineers, 110

Employer or employed?, 38; *see also* private or public service

Engineers, 15–19, 25–6

Environmental planning, 21–2, 60, 69, 73; *see also* landscape architects

Estate management, 22

European Economic Community, *see* Common Market

Evening classes, 100

Examinations, RIBA, 53–4, 98, 100; *see also* external examinations

Expansion in business, 105–6

Experience, how to get, 103
Experiments in new designs, 80–1
External examinations, 101–2; *see also* examinations, RIBA
Extras not called for in original plans, 119

Factories, 14, 18, 26, 77
Fame: shall I be famous?, 91–2
Fashion, following, 13
Fee-percentages, why they do not make for extravagance, 89
Fees: for alterations, 89; scale of, 46, 55, 80, 88–9; 6 per cent rule, 88; Spanish system of determining, 91; when in private service, 30
Fellowships, *see* FRIBA
Finals, 100–1
Fire regulations, 28, 116
Flexibility in space utilisation, a problem of the future, 130
Following in father's footsteps, 64
Fortunes *can* be made, 85
Forward planning, a must in an architect's armoury, 114–15
FRIBA, 83–4
Furnishings, 27
Future prospects (post 1974), 121–34

GCE standards required, 100
Goodwill, fostering, 120
Greater London Council, *see* London County Council
Group-working during training, 98

Heating, 26, 110
Hertfordshire experiment in interchangeable standard parts, 125–6
Horizontal work structure, 33
Hospitals, 20, 26, 37
Hotels, 26, 36
Houses, privately purpose built, 79–81
Housing, 14, 18, 25, 31, 34, 37–8

Imitations, vulgar, 45
Improvements in standards, the need to be able to suggest, 44–5
Individuality in design, 36–7
Industrial companies, architects serving, 37
Industrial Revolution, 15–16
Institutions and Organisations, list of British, 138–40
Insurance companies, architects serving, 37
Interior design, 27, 78
Intermediate examination, 100–1
International standards, tendency towards, 127
International Union of Architects, 52, 127
Iron and steel, 15
IUA, *see* International Union of Architects

Job security *see* security in job
Jobs: costing overheads for each, 80; ready for tender, 117; *see also* projects

Keay, Sir Lancelot, 35–6

Ladders, climbing of, 63
Land, economic use of, 46, 110
Landscape architects, 26–7, 78, 110
Learning from fellow students, 101–2
Liaison Committee of Architects of the Common Market, 128; see also Common Market
Librarian, 107
Licentiates, see LRIBA
Lighting, 26
Live projects, as a teaching aid, 97, 103–4
Local Government, architects serving in, 18, 22, 31, 74; see also London County Council
London County Council, example of architects then employed by, 32–4, 38
LRIBA, 83–4
Lyons, Eric, 45

Masons, 13
Mathematics, is knowledge of needed?, 65–6
Matthew, Sir Robert, 33
Memberships, see MRIBA
Men of power, are they men of taste?, 48
Metrication, 127
Model-making, 108
Monopolies Commission, 90
Motor cars, 70
MRIBA, 84
Multi-storey versus single, 20

New Towns, 21, 37, 78–9

O- and A-level subjects required, 100
Observation, need to have good powers of, 65, 103
Offices: blocks, 20, 47, 77; boy, duties of, 107–8; design of, 42, 45–6; management of, 98; overheads for, 80–1; typical architects', 105–20
Old buildings, campaign against pulling down of, 61
Old buildings, study of, for conversion, 78
One-man-band businesses, 106
Opportunities open to architects, 76–92
Order out of chaos, need to create, 65
Organisations and Institutes, list of British, 138–40
Overheads in the office, 80–1

Package deals, 121–4
Partnerships, 29, 51
Pension, 33
Percentage of buildings where no architect employed, 24n
Photographing of projects, 119; see also colour slides
Planning officers, see town planning
Planning permission, 25
Prefabricated components, 41, 125–6; see also standard parts, interchangeable
Preservationism, 61–2
Printing, a cause of delay, 108–9
Printing machine, 108

Private or public service ?, 30–43
Private practice, 30–43
Prizes, 42, 50; see also competitions
Professional institutes, 18, 138–40
Professional Practice Examination (incl office management), 98; see also examinations
Professional Services Board, see under RIBA
Professional status, 14, 44–62; see also Code of Professional Conduct
Projects: abandoned, fees for, 88; sequence of operations in any one, 114–20; type of, proceeding in a typical office, 109–10
Promotion, 33
Property developers, architects serving, 37, 47
Property Services Agency, 19, 87
Prospects in profession, 121–34
Public service, 30–43
Public Works Departments, 19, 87
Pupilage system (outdated), 40, 93

Qualifications, 39
Qualities in an architect, 63–75
Quantity Surveyors, 27–8, 52, 110, 118

Railway stations, 14
Reduced fees, circumstances demanding, 88–9
Refresher courses, 102–3
Registration as architect, see architects under Registration Act
Regulations, building, 116

Repetitive work, reduced fees for, 88–9
Research, 21, 126–7
Restaurants, 27
Rewards open to architects, 76–92
RIBA, see Royal Institute of British Architects
Royal Charter (1837), 14, 54
Royal Fine Art Commission (and Act, 1922), 58–60, 79
Royal Institute of British Architects (RIBA) (mentioned), 14, 36, 42, 46, 49, 52–8, 83; architects need not be members of, 53–4; contract form, 118; financial crisis of 1972, 56; library at, 54; members of council of, 56; monthly journal of, 54; Professional Services Board, 55; statement of aims of, 54; subscriptions to, 56–7
Royal Society, 14
Rules, RIBA's for competitions, see competitions
Running costs (in office), 80–1

Salary, when in public service, 30, 55
School fees when training, 100
School of Environmental Studies, 99, 129; of Tropical Architecture, 129; of Architecture, see architectural schools
Schools, building of, 31–4
Scientific Institutions, 26, 138–40
Secretaries, duties of, 107
Security in job, 86–7; see also work-flow, irregularity in

Self-employed or salaried, 30–1
Shadows, as an aid to three-dimensional drawings, 95
Shops, 27, 36, 77
Site visits, 108, 115, 119
Skiing, 70
Sociology, 22
Span Company, 45
Specialisation, 15–16, 37, 72, 76–9; *see also* consultancy
Specialist or Jack-of-all-trades, 31–2
Specifications, 110, 116
Sports where architects most excel, 70
Standard parts, interchangeable, 41, 125–6
Standards of comfort, architect's job to improve, 46
Stephenson, Robert, 16
Structural engineers, 26
Student training, 93–104
Studying for architecture, 93–104; (up to 1950, 93–7, after 97–104)
Success, what leads to commercial, 64–5
Summerson, Sir John, 71
Surveying, 22, 110–11

Teams of architects, tendency towards, 39, 130
Telford, Thomas, 16
Tenders, 117–18
Three-dimensional views, must be able to visualise, 65, 94
Time sheets, 80
Town and Country Planning Act (1947), 22

Town Halls, 77–8
Town Planning: 21–5, 34; degrees in, 78
Training, programme, of, 98
Travelling expenses, 89
Two-stage competitions, *see* competitions

Under-estimates, 117
Unprofessional practices, 57
Urban development, *see* town planning
Use-zoning, 23

Vacancies in Architecture, *see* architects *under* supply of
Vanbrugh, Sir John, 14
Variations to original drawings, 89; *see also* extras
Variety in employment, 37–8
Ventilation, 26, 129
Vertical work structure, 33
Viaducts, 16
Vintage cars, 70

Women as architects, 63–4
Work-flow, irregularity in, 51, 86, 89
Working area, architect's need to know history of, 73
Works, clerks of, *see* Clerks of Works
World War II, effects of, 34–5
Wren, Sir Christopher, 14, 31, 33, 71

Zoning, *see* use-zoning